WHY WOULD ANYONE
BELIEVE IN GOD?

COGNITIVE SCIENCE OF RELIGION SERIES

Series Editors: **HARVEY WHITEHOUSE** and **LUTHER H. MARTIN**

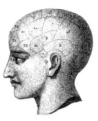

The Cognitive Science of Religion Series publishes research into the cognitive foundations of religious thinking and behavior and their consequences for social morphology. The emphasis of the series is on scientific approaches to the study of religion within the framework of the cognitive sciences, including experimental, clinical, or laboratory studies, but works drawing upon ethnographic, linguistic, archaeological, or historical research are welcome, as are critical appraisals of research in these areas. In addition to providing a forum for presenting new empirical evidence and major theoretical innovations, the series publishes concise overviews of issues in the field suitable for students and general readers. The series is published in cooperation with the Institute for Cognition and Culture at Queen's University, Belfast.

TITLES IN THE SERIES:

Modes of Religiosity: A Cognitive Theory of Religious Transmission
By Harvey Whitehouse

Magic, Miracles, and Religion: A Scientist's Perspective
By Ilkka Pyysiäinen

Why Would Anyone Believe in God?
By Justin L. Barrett

Ritual and Memory: Towards a Comparative Anthropology of Religion
Edited by Harvey Whitehouse and James Laidlaw

Theorizing Religions Past: Archaeology, History, and Cognition
Edited by Harvey Whitehouse and Luther H. Martin

How the Bible Works: An Anthropological Study of Evangelical Biblicism
By Brian E. Malley

FORTHCOMING TITLES:

Mind and Religion: Psychological and Cognitive Foundations of Religion
Edited by Harvey Whitehouse and Robert N. McCauley

The Evolution of Religion
By Harvey Whitehouse

God from the Machine
By William Sims Bainbridge

WHY WOULD ANYONE BELIEVE IN GOD?

JUSTIN L. BARRETT

A Division of
ROWMAN & LITTLEFIELD PUBLISHERS, INC.
Lanham • Boulder • New York • Toronto • Plymouth, UK

ALTAMIRA PRESS
A division of Rowman & Littlefield Publishers, Inc.
4501 Forbes Boulevard, Suite 200
Lanham, MD 20706

Estover Road
Plymouth PL6 7PY
United Kingdon

British Library Cataloguing in Publication Information Available

Library of Congress Cataloging-in-Publication Data
Barrett, Justin L., 1971–
   Why would anyone believe in God? / Justin L. Barrett.
      p. cm. — (Cognitive science of religion series)
   Includes bibliographical references and index.
   ISBN 0-7591-0666-5 (alk. paper) — ISBN 0-7591-0667-3 (pbk. : alk. paper)
      1. Faith—Psychology. 2. Psychology, Religious. I. Title. II. Series.

BL53.B335 2004
212—dc22   2003024268

Printed in the United States of America

∞™ The paper used in this publication meets the minimum requirements of American National Standard for Information Sciences—Permanence of Paper for Printed Library Materials, ANSI/NISO Z39.48–1992.

Contents

Preface

IN OCTOBER 2002, I spoke at a conference at Harvard University titled "Why Would Anyone Believe in God?" Though some who attended believed in God and wondered "why not?" I sensed that the vast majority of this large audience of political scientists, economists, psychologists, anthropologists, sociologists, and philosophers filled the lecture hall because they found belief in God perplexing. As the conference organizer suggested and members of the presenting panel and audience reiterated throughout the day, why *indeed* believe in the existence of a being for whom there is no scientific evidence, who cannot be proven to (or proven not to) exist, and whose existence produces numerous logical impossibilities? Time and again, participants spoke of the utter irrationality of religious beliefs.

Using the latest cognitive and psychological scientific data and theory, this book answers the question "why would anyone believe in God?" As will become evident, I agree with the conference organizer and participants that this question deserves an answer. It will also become evident that I do not regard belief in God as strange, loony, or irrational. Indeed, once examined from a scientific perspective, both believers and nonbelievers should appreciate how very natural and almost inevitable widespread religious belief is. What follows is my argument in a nutshell.

By virtue of our biological endowment as human beings and our environmental endowment from living in this world, people all over the world have similar minds. Regardless of culture, people tend to have minds with many basic structures that perform numerous mundane tasks, such as discerning the objects around us, defining those objects, and observing how those objects causally interact. Operating largely without our awareness, mental "tools" encourage us to think similarly about many banal features of the world around us. These mental tools also encourage people to think about and believe in gods, the Judeo-Christian God enjoying particularly favorable treatment, especially during child development. Once introduced into a population, belief in the existence of a supreme god with properties such as being superknowing, superpowerful, and immortal is highly contagious and a hard habit to break. The way our minds are structured and develop make these beliefs very attractive.

I make this central argument in the first six chapters. Understanding why one believes in God first requires understanding why one believes in anything. If we can't understand why people believe in gravity or in the existence of objects such as chairs or other people's minds, how can we understand belief in God? In chapter 1, I lay out a framework for understanding the nature of belief and how people come to believe in anything, let alone God. Perhaps the most technical chapter of the book, I beg the reader's patience. A thorough understanding of the ideas presented in chapter 1 is not necessary for understanding the main points of the book, but a cursory introduction helps considerably.

Chapters 2, 3, and 4 make the case that concepts of gods (generally) arise and spread readily because of the strong support of mental tools found in minds the world over. Our minds pay special attention to the things I call agents: thinking, feeling, intentional beings. Agents we think about include people, animals (especially our dear pets), ghosts, goblins, and gods. Our minds tend to consider and believe in agents that have a limited set of superhuman properties. Not only do mental structures enable religious ideas centered on agents to be easily acquired, but religious ideas would not be the way they are if not for the *constraints* mental structures impose on the formation and transmission of these conceptions of gods.

In chapter 5, I sketch ways in which existing religious practices reinforce religious belief. Different types of ceremonies and rituals impact the spread of religious beliefs in importantly different ways.

Chapter 6 turns from religious concepts and belief in gods generally to why people might believe in God particularly. Largely because of the way human minds develop regardless of culture, children's minds may find acquiring ideas about a god being superpowerful, superknowing, superperceiving, and immortal is especially easy.

Having answered "why would anyone believe in God?" in the first six chapters, in chapter 7, I try to amplify the argument by comparing the belief in God to the belief that other people have minds. I describe how both types of belief arise through comparable mental processes. Consequently, believing in God may be as natural as believing that other people have beliefs, desires, thoughts, and ideas.

If believing in gods and God comes so easily and is so natural, why do some fail to believe? In chapter 8, I offer a skeletal explanation for why atheism occurs and under what conditions. Chapter 9 attempts to answer a few lingering questions.

I emphasize that this account for belief in God is largely a tale of *selection*. Often we think that cultural ideas (such as religious ones) can be explained simply by appealing to what was taught by a cultural group: Mary believes in God because Pastor John told her to. But why does Pastor John believe? Because Pastor Jim told him. But why does Pastor Jim believe? As you can see, this doesn't explain anything. Culture cannot explain culture, and religion cannot explain religion. Rather, my strategy for explaining belief in gods generally and God particularly is to identify those factors that make these beliefs attractive to human minds and that are likely to be understood, remembered, believed, and passed on more so than other ideas.

My hope is that this book will be useful to a broad audience. I assume no specialized knowledge from readers. Believers in God might discover in this book a more thorough understanding of the processes that contribute to their belief. Nonbelievers might find that the minds of religious people are not so inexplicable after all. For psychologists and cognitive scientists, this book might serve as an introduction to the scientific study of religion. For anthropologists, it may serve as an appetizer for how the sciences of the mind are relevant to cultural materials. Theologians and scientists interested in how the behavioral and evolutionary sciences bear on religious belief could also find food for thought.

Of course, targeting such a diverse readership carries some dangers. I have tried to minimize technical features without losing precision—a difficult balancing act. Likewise, I have attempted to produce a clear, parsimonious explanation of religious belief without trivializing the complexities of religion. Finally, I have struggled to keep this book brief so that too many unfamiliar notions are not presented at once. Naturally, brevity requires omitting some fascinating topics. My apologies if I have left out your favorites.

This book represents the culmination of my work in the cognitive science of religion over the past ten years, supported in part by the generous support of the John Templeton Foundation. But many of the ideas presented here draw on the insights and expertise of a group of colleagues with whom I have enjoyed numerous productive exchanges (and a few disagreements) over the years. I am indebted to Pascal Boyer, Tom Lawson, Brian Malley, Luther Martin, Bob McCauley, Rebekah Richert, and Harvey Whitehouse for their collegiality over the years and for feedback on the ideas presented here. I am grateful to Michael Jump and especially my wife, Sherry Barrett, for thorough commentary on early drafts. Their careful eyes have greatly improved the final product. I thank Paul Harris, Frank Keil, Deborah Kelemen, Henry Wellman, and Nicholas Wolterstorff for prodding me to get off my duff and start writing. Without their encouragement, this book might have forever remained thoughts in one man's head. Finally, I thank my wife and children, Skylar and Sierra, for their support and forbearance.

What Does It Mean to "Believe"? I

THROUGH THE AGES and around the world, people have believed in various gods. While some scholars and nonbelievers find such beliefs mystifying, to those who hold them, nothing seems peculiar or unnatural about belief. In fact, until confronted with others who don't believe in religious entities, believing goes on unnoticed. To many believers, questions such as "do you believe in spirits?" or "do you believe in God?" make about as much sense as "do you believe in food?" or "do you believe in people?" What makes religious belief so natural and commonplace for some but so odd for others? To address the reasons people hold the sorts of religious beliefs they do, including belief in God, we must first have some sense for how people come about believing anything at all.

For most educated, thinking people, how we go about forming beliefs may seem rather straightforward. We carefully, logically evaluate evidence for and against a particular claim, and if the evidence outweighs counterexplanations, we believe the claim to be true. If only it were that simple. Though philosophers and scientists present logical evaluation of evidence as an ideal for forming beliefs, in practice, most beliefs we hold—even those of philosophers and scientists—arise through less transparent means.

We use the words *belief* and *believe* in many different ways. Sometimes believing something implies a strong commitment to something being true, as in "I believe racism is wrong." Sometimes believing suggests weak commitment, as in "I believe it will rain today." Sometimes believing suggests trusting another person, as in "I believe in my wife's faithfulness." People invoke these and other senses of "belief" when speaking about God. They believe God exists, they *believe* God approves of their behavior but don't *know* it, and they believe in God's love.

I

Regardless of nuance, belief is fundamentally a mental process. Individuals use their minds to believe or disbelieve. Consequently, before explaining why anyone would believe in God, explaining the psychology of how it is that people *believe* is in order. Understanding where beliefs generally come from is critical to understanding why people believe in God. In this chapter, I will share some thoughts on the psychology of everyday beliefs that all people make day in and day out. The rest of this book builds on this foundation.

Two Types of Belief

Behind the many ways people use the term *believe* are two types of belief derived from two different types of mental activity. I will term one kind of belief *reflective* and the other *nonreflective*.[1] Briefly, reflective beliefs are those we arrive at through conscious, deliberate contemplation or explicit instruction. We reflectively believe many facts, such as that cars run on gasoline, that $12 \times 8 = 96$, that caterpillars turn into butterflies, and that George Washington was the first president of the United States. We reflectively believe matters of opinion, such as that mother is a great cook or that blue is a nicer color for clothing than orange. By reflective beliefs, I mean the class of beliefs we commonly refer to as "beliefs," including belief in God. But many, if not most, of our reflective beliefs, including belief in God, arise from and are supported by nonreflective beliefs.

Nonreflective beliefs are those that come automatically, require no careful rumination, and seem to arise instantaneously and sometimes even "against better judgment." These nonreflective beliefs are terribly important for successfully functioning in the day-to-day world. Consider the following nonreflective beliefs:

- When I am hungry, I should eat.
- I can't walk directly through a solid wall.
- My children want things I don't want them to want.
- If I throw a rock in the air, it will come back down.

We hold these and countless other mundane beliefs nonreflectively. We don't need to consider them consciously. Such beliefs operate continually in the background, freeing our conscious minds to deal with other thoughts. Nonreflective beliefs are so ubiquitous and so often nonconscious that we frequently are not aware they are there.[2]

Suppose you were in a park flanked by a forest and saw a dull-brown, furry thing about the size of a loaf of bread moving along the tree line. Having never seen the thing before, you already have a number of beliefs about it without any careful contemplation. Relying only on intuitions, you believe it is an animal, don't you? (It could have been a machine covered with faux fur.) Do you think it was born? If it had babies, would they be the same type of animal? Does it eat? Breathe? If a dog ran toward it, what would it do? If you threw it in the air, would it fall? If you threw it against a wall, would it pass through? If you are like most people, you could answer nearly all these questions with a fair amount of confidence and without much, if any, consideration. These beliefs are nonreflective. But where do nonreflective beliefs come from, and how do they relate to reflective beliefs, particularly belief in God? To further unpack this distinction between reflective and nonreflective beliefs so that it may be helpful for understanding religious beliefs, a brief journey into the structure and functioning of the human mind is necessary.

The Mind as a Workshop

Thinking of the human mind as a workshop filled with racks of tools may be helpful. A lot of work happens in our minds. Cognitive scientists (scholars who study the activities of the mind) have concluded that the adult human mind has a large number of devices that are used for different problems on different occasions.[3] Thus, for instance, the brain has specialized tools for tackling the interpretation and production of language, other tools for processing information picked up through the eyes, and other tools for making sense of other people's behaviors. Cognitive scientists debate whether some parts of the brain end up being used as more than one tool (or parts of more than one tool), analogous to how a standard hammer can be used as more than one tool (such as for pounding as well as pulling nails); how many tools the brain possesses; and whether these tools arise primarily from our biological makeup or whether they develop primarily through experience. The notion that the adult human brain possesses an array of specialized tools is scarcely debated anymore. Instead of having one powerful multipurpose mental tool, we have a number of specialized ones.

Most of these *mental tools* operate automatically, without any conscious awareness. They efficiently and rapidly solve lots of problems without concentration or angst, much the same way that computer programs solve problems in a swift, effortless fashion. Thus, when we confront an object, such as the previously mentioned fuzzy thing, one mental tool, the *object detection device*, recognizes it as an object and passes on this nonreflective belief to a number of other mental tools, including the *animal identifier* and the *object describer*. The animal identifier takes the information about the object's size, coloring, texture, movement, and location and arrives at the nonreflective belief that the thing is indeed an animal. The animal identifier passes this nonreflective belief on to yet other mental tools, such as the *living-thing describer*, which nonreflectively believes that the animal in question eats, breathes, and produces similar offspring, among other bits of information. The object describer, having been activated by the object detection device, nonreflectively believes that the thing likewise has all the properties of a normal, bounded, physical object. For instance, it falls to the earth when unsupported and cannot pass directly through other solid objects.[4]

It may be helpful to think of these tools as falling into three categories: categorizers, describers, and facilitators. *Categorizers* are mental tools that receive information primarily from our basic senses (hearing, smelling, seeing, tasting, and touching) and use that information to determine what sort of thing or things we have perceived. For example, on the basis of the visual appearance of something, we might decide that it is a bounded object (such as a ball) or that it is a fluid or formless substance (such as water). Such determination is typically done instantaneously without awareness because of the operation of the object detection device. This device is almost certainly active at birth. At birth, infants also have a *face detector*, which is used to discern human faces from the environment. Such a device enables babies only one day old to imitate the facial expressions of others, even before they have seen, or presumably know they have, their own face.[5] Other categorizers determine whether an object (once identified as such by the object detection device) is an animal, a plant, a human-made thing, and so forth. Perhaps the most important tool for the present discussion in the categorizer group is the *agency detection device*. This tool looks for evidence of beings (such as people or animals) that not merely respond to their environment but also initiate action on the basis of their own internal states, such as beliefs and desires.

Describers are devices that our minds automatically use for supposing the properties of any given object or thing once it has been identified by a categorizer.[6] For instance, whenever a baby (or an adult) recognizes something as an object—whether a rock or ball or cat or unknown thing—it automatically assumes that the thing has all the properties of a bounded object: occupying a single location at a time, not being able to pass through other solid objects, being subject to gravity, being movable through contact, requiring time to move from one place to another, and so forth.[7] The object describer generates all these property-related expectations even if the particular object in question is unfamiliar. The living-thing describer automatically ascribes nutritional needs, growth, death, and the ability to reproduce its own kind to those things categorized as animals. Though no firm evidence exists that the living-thing describer operates in infancy, it seems to be functional by around age five.[8] The agent describer, better known as the Theory of Mind (ToM), kicks into action once the agency detection device recognizes something that seems to initiate its own actions and does not merely respond mechanistically to environmental factors. The ToM then attributes a host of mental properties to the agent in question—percepts that enable it to negotiate the environment, desires that motivate actions, thoughts and beliefs that guide actions, memory for storing percepts and thoughts, and so forth.[9]

The third group of tools may be called *facilitators*. The function of facilitators results primarily in coordinating social activity and other behaviors that depend on the situation and not merely on the identity of the things involved. Facilitators help people understand and predict human behavior in specific situations that require more explanation than appealing to simple beliefs and desires (the job of the ToM). Three facilitators may be particularly important for explaining religious beliefs. First, a *social exchange regulator* tries to make sense of who owes what to whom for what reason.[10] Second, a *social status monitor* attempts to determine the high-status members of a group with whom it would be important to form alliances or from whom it would be profitable to learn and imitate.[11] Third, an *intuitive morality tool*, used in both social and nonsocial settings, helps people function in social settings, such as when they agree to certain behavioral norms even without explicit reasons for doing so.[12] Table 1.1 lists some mental tools that I will use in subsequent chapters.

Categorizers, describers, and facilitators have a number of features in common. All are mental tools that operate implicitly and automatically. The fluidity with which they solve problems renders them largely invisible to conscious reflection or evaluation. These tools also seem to be present in all adult populations regardless of culture (though facilitators may have more variability than categorizers or describers). Thus, these tools are factors that might help account for cross-cultural or recurrent features of human thought and behavior, such as beliefs in gods and God.

That people the world over possess these mental tools does not necessarily mean that such tools are biologically "hardwired" into our brains or that their development is inevitable. For the present discussion, I will remain largely agnostic on these issues. However, the classes of tools do have some differences in development, which sometimes suggests differences in the contribution of "nature" versus "nurture" in their emergence. Research indicates that infants and sometimes newborns possess well-developed categorizers, including the object detection device, the agency detection device, and a face detector. Some research has provided evidence that animal and artifact identifiers function in the first two years of life.[13]

Table 1.1 Mental Tools

Categorizers	Describers	Facilitators
Object detection device	Object describer	Social exchange regulator
Agency detection device	Living-thing describer	Social status monitor
Face detector	Theory of Mind	Intuitive morality
Animal identifier	Artifact describer	
Artifact identifier		

Describers, however, seem to emerge somewhat later in development and take longer to reach adultlike maturity. The ToM, for instance, may have its origins in the first three years of life but does not consistently approximate how adults reason until age four or older. A similar developmental pace appears to operate for other describers. Finally, many facilitators seem to come into their own only in middle childhood through adulthood. If so, this general developmental pattern would not be surprising because it reflects important functional relationships between the three types of tools: facilitators typically require that a certain amount of description has taken place, and describers assume categorization. To illustrate, social exchange regulation assumes that the beings who engage in the exchange relationship have beliefs, desires, memory, and experiences attributed by the ToM (a describer). The mind activates the ToM in cases in which an object is identified as an agent—the role of the agency detection device (a categorizer).

The Origin and Features of Nonreflective Beliefs

Now that some basic architecture of the mind is in hand, I can return to the nature of belief. In my description of the various tools, it may have sounded as if these tools are little people in our heads forming their own beliefs. Such a metaphor would capture the essentials well enough, for these mental tools produce nonreflective beliefs. When Mary's object detection device registers some visual patterns as a bounded physical object in front of her, she experiences a nonreflective belief that an object is in front of her. When Juan sees Mike take an apple from a tree and eat it, Juan's ToM interprets Mike's action as the result of Mike's desire to eat the apple. Thus, Juan experiences a nonreflective belief that Mike desired the apple.

When developmental psychologists claim that infants believe that objects in motion tend to continue on inertial paths, they refer to the nonreflective beliefs of infants. Such beliefs come from the object describer. When scientists who examine the interactions of people and computers say that people believe that computers have feelings (or have sinister plans to make our lives miserable), generally they refer to nonreflective beliefs generated by people's agency detection device and ToM working together to try to make sense of computers.

Mental tools—operating without our awareness—constantly produce nonreflective beliefs. Producing such beliefs is the job of these tools, and the utility of having such mental tools "instinctively" make decisions and form beliefs cannot be underestimated. What if every time we move an object from one place to another (as when we feed ourselves, get dressed, wash dishes, and so forth) we had to reason consciously that objects require support, or else they fall toward the ground until their path is blocked by another physical object of sufficient density to stop their descent? Isn't it much more convenient that we have an unconscious device that forms beliefs about how gravity operates on objects so that we don't have to clutter our conscious mind with such mundane issues?

Perhaps you have noticed that all my examples of nonreflective belief rely on nonverbal behavioral evidence to support the belief. Babies' nonreflective beliefs about objects become clear by examining (very carefully) their subtle behaviors. Adults' belief that computers have minds and feelings comes to light primarily under experimental scrutiny of nonverbal behaviors and indirect verbal behaviors. By these examples I do not mean to imply that verbal evidence for nonreflective beliefs does not exist. Rather, nonreflective beliefs typically do not impinge enough on conscious activity to merit verbal commentary. When verbal evidence is available, it is indirect, such as when people say, "This stupid machine!" in reference to their computer, not direct, as when saying, "I do believe this computer has beliefs and desires that exceed its programming in a way that disturbs me."

The Origins and Features of Reflective Beliefs

In addition to automatic mental tools that function without awareness to produce nonreflective beliefs, people also enjoy powerful conscious mental abilities. Psychologists sometimes refer to these conscious mental tools as "higher-order" or "executive" functions of the mind or *metarepresentational devices*. What all these terms point to is the ability to evaluate information reflectively and to come to a decision that might not agree with our first, automatic impulses. When we stop to think things over, weigh the pros and cons, examine the evidence for and against, and then make a decision to believe or disbelieve a claim, our reflective abilities are working.

Differences between Reflective and Nonreflective Beliefs

By "reflective beliefs," I refer to beliefs arrived at through conscious, deliberate mental activity. Perhaps closer to what we commonly think of as "beliefs," reflective beliefs contrast with nonreflective beliefs on a number of fronts. First, whereas nonreflective beliefs come rapidly and automatically from mental tools, reflective beliefs take relatively more time to form. Believing that Moses wrote or edited the bulk of the Pentateuch might take several years of college study to decide. That would be a slow-forming belief. Other reflective beliefs, such as that it will rain today, might require only a quick glance out of the window. Nevertheless, even these very fast-forming reflective beliefs require more time to develop than nonreflective beliefs.

A second way in which reflective beliefs differ from nonreflective beliefs is the contexts in which they arise and are used. Nonreflective beliefs seem to spontaneously generate in each and every mundane moment. Reflective beliefs typically surface when a decision or judgment evidently has to be made, that is, when a problem is deliberately presented that requires a solution. Nonreflective beliefs form simply by looking at the world around us. Reflective beliefs form from wondering what to do about the world around us. What would be best to make for dinner? How will I go about getting to work today? Why should I agree to my neighbor's request? Though sometimes mundane, the contexts in which reflective beliefs are needed make the contexts of most nonreflective beliefs—such as setting down a spoon or walking through a doorway—pale by comparison in their complexity and novelty.

Unlike nonreflective beliefs, people present direct verbal evidence for their reflective beliefs. They may simply state what they believe. "I think dogs are better pets than cats," someone might say. Or "I believe that Marxism is damaging to individual motivation." Or "that man has a bag of magical potions that could change you into a tarantula." This explicit, verbal reporting of reflective beliefs makes those beliefs obvious and easy to gauge—but not always. Sometimes reports of one's own beliefs may be deceptive, but more frequently, people do not have a reflective belief until asked for one. To illustrate, when asked whether I believe that spring will come early this year, I might have previously formed no belief one way or another. But once asked, I may try to reason through the problem to come up with a belief.

Perhaps a more interesting feature of reflective beliefs and their verbal reports is that verbal reports of beliefs, even when sincerely held, may have little correspondence with relevant behaviors. Previously I mentioned that to determine nonreflective beliefs, observers must examine behaviors. In the case of reflective beliefs, little correspondence between beliefs and behaviors may exist. The case of "beautyism" is an example. The reflective belief, verbally reported, that "beauty is only skin deep" does not correspond to the strongly documented tendency for people to overestimate the intellectual and social abilities of physically attractive children as compared with less attractive children.[14] Much racist thinking—sincerely denounced by the practitioners—also illustrates this dissociation between reflective belief and behavior, as when a couple claim that people of all races should be treated the same but then have a negative visceral reaction to the suggestion that their child might marry someone from a different race.[15]

A final difference between reflective and nonreflective beliefs worth noting is their differences in cultural relativity. As I will explain later in this chapter, reflective beliefs are shaped and heavily informed by nonconscious mental tools (via nonreflective beliefs). Nevertheless, because reflective beliefs may include elements verbally communicated or drawn from personal experience, reflective beliefs vary from individual to individual and from cultural group to cultural group. Nonreflective beliefs, being closely tied to mental tools that appear and function essentially the same in everyone, show little variation from place to place or from person to person. It follows that those reflective beliefs that arise most directly from nonreflective beliefs would likewise show little interpersonal or intercultural variation. For example, no matter where you go or to whom you talk, people believe that rocks can be in only one place at a time, cannot pass directly through other solid objects, and must be supported or else fall downward.

Reliability of Reflective and Nonreflective Beliefs

Note that the fact that a belief is reflective or nonreflective has no direct relationship to the belief being true or false. Though reflective beliefs may arise through careful, systematic evaluation of evidence, mistakes in reasoning or inadequacies of evidence may lead to erroneous conclusions. Indeed, reflective beliefs include the domains of opinion and preference. Nonreflective beliefs often correspond nicely to reality. This reliability comes from the observation that the mental tools responsible for these beliefs exist in large part because of their contribution to human survival throughout time. For instance, if people didn't automatically reason in a way that was mostly accurate about physical objects, they would probably spend much more time dropping things on each other's heads and falling off cliffs than they currently do. Nevertheless, these devices are tuned to survival and not to the firm establishment of truth. What mental tools provide is quick "best guesses" as to the identity and properties of objects and how to explain cause-and-effect relationships. These best guesses sometimes prove inaccurate. I discuss this issue further in the next chapter. Table 1.2 compares features of reflective and nonreflective beliefs.

Table 1.2 Reflective versus Nonreflective Beliefs

Reflective Beliefs	Nonreflective Beliefs
Consciously/explicitly held	May or may not be conscious or explicit
Produced deliberately and often slowly	Produced automatically and rapidly
Draw on outputs of many mental tools and memories	Produced by one or a small number of related mental tools
Best evidence of belief is typically explicit statements that may or may not be consistent with relevant behaviors	Best evidence of belief is typically behavioral
May or may not be empirically verifiable	May or may not be empirically verifiable
May or may not be rationally justifiable	May or may not be rationally justifiable
May or may not be true	May or may not be true
Great potential for within-group variation	Typically strong within-group uniformity

Religious Beliefs and the
Reflective/Nonreflective Distinction

When people think about or discuss religious beliefs, they usually consider reflective religious beliefs. Though these explicit religious beliefs capture the attention of theologians, pastors, and social scientists, religious beliefs come in both flavors. Some are reflective, such as believing that "God exists as three persons" and that "God desires peace on earth," and some are nonreflective, such as believing that "God has desires" and that "God perceives human actions." Despite their mundane qualities, nonreflective beliefs do a tremendous amount of work in filling out religious beliefs, motivating behaviors, and making the fancier theological notions possible. For instance, that our ToM tool automatically attributes desires to God enables discussions about what exactly God's desires might be. Nonreflective beliefs that God perceives human actions make discussions of God's judgments regarding sin possible. When people reflectively talk about or engage in prayer, they nonreflectively believe that God can both perceive and understand human language (particularly our own language). All folk theology and religious practices gain structure and support from nonreflective beliefs.[16]

Nonreflective religious beliefs sometimes contradict reflective religious beliefs. For instance, a small number of Christians argue that people's behaviors and attitudes are completely within God's control and that people do not have any free will. Nevertheless, in their day-to-day activity, these same Christians certainly behave as if they believe in free will. If their child transgresses, it sure isn't God's fault. ToM registers a strong nonreflective belief that people possess freedom to act on the basis of one's own desires. Consequently, consistently believing a strong doctrine denying free will presents formidable difficulties. Similarly, many properties of God embraced reflectively may contradict an individual's nonreflective beliefs.

In a series of experiments, I examined reflective beliefs about God's properties compared with nonreflective beliefs on the same dimensions.[17] I asked theists (from many world religions) and nontheists in the United States and northern India whether God possesses a number of properties. (For Hindu participants in India, I used the names of several Indian deities). Across all groups sampled, God was attributed such nonhuman properties as being able to pay attention to multiple activities at the same time, not having a single location but being either everywhere or nowhere, not needing to hear or see to know about things, being able to read minds, and so forth. People's reflective beliefs about God fairly closely matched the exotic theological properties many world religions embrace and teach. When these same individuals recalled or paraphrased sketchy accounts of God's activities, however, they systematically misremembered God as having human properties in contradiction to these theological ones.

A well-substantiated body of research on memory for narratives shows that what gets remembered or comprehended is a combination of the text and the concepts or beliefs brought to the reading of the text. Thus, a good measure of nonreflective concepts is the type of intrusion errors (or inserted information) that a reader remembers (incorrectly) as being part of a text. I carefully constructed the narratives used in these studies so that readers could remember the stories using either "theologically correct" concepts of God or less orthodox humanlike concepts. Though the participants reflectively affirmed the theologically correct concepts, their nonreflective concepts remained largely anthropomorphic. That is, when reasoning about God using God's properties instead of reflecting on and reporting God's properties, these same individuals nonreflectively used human properties to characterize God. These properties included being able to pay attention to only one thing at a time, moving from one location to another, having only one particular location in space and time, and needing to hear and see things to know about them.

People seem to have difficulty maintaining the integrity of their reflective theological concepts in rapid, real-time problem solving because of processing demands. Theological properties, such as being able to be in multiple places at once, not needing to perceive, being able to attend to an infinite number of problems at once, and not being bound by time, importantly deviate from the nonreflective beliefs that mental tools freely generate. As such, these reflectively held concepts are more difficult to use rapidly than nonreflective beliefs. Nonconscious mental tools are not accustomed to handling such fancy concepts and find them cumbersome. Thus, when presented with accounts of God (or other equally complicated concepts, such as those in quantum physics) that must be rapidly comprehended and remembered, most of the features that do not enjoy the strong support of mental tools get replaced by simpler, nonreflective versions that can produce rapid inferences, predictions, and explanations.

These findings from the narrative comprehension tasks nicely illustrate how reflective religious beliefs sometimes contradict or at least depart from nonreflective religious beliefs. This divergence arises in part because nonreflective beliefs are not typically available to conscious access and are not easily altered because they are directly produced by nonconscious mental tools. The occasional difference between these two classes of beliefs should not, however, be taken to mean that nonreflective and reflective beliefs operate independently.

The Relationship between Reflective and Nonreflective Beliefs

In many cases, reflective beliefs arise as the consequence of verbal discourse, as when one person persuades another person of the truth of some claim. More frequently, reflective beliefs arise in large part because of related nonreflective beliefs influencing the conscious assessment of possible beliefs. In the following sections, I identify three related ways in which nonreflective beliefs influence the formation of reflective beliefs. First, nonreflective beliefs serve as default options for reflective beliefs. Second, reflective beliefs that resonate with nonreflective beliefs seem more plausible. Finally, nonreflective beliefs shape experiences that we consciously use as evidence to form reflective beliefs.

Nonreflective Beliefs Act as Defaults for Reflective Beliefs

If I presented a group of unschooled people with an object (such as a type of rock) that they had never seen before and asked them if they believed it would fall to the earth when I released it from support, the vast majority of the group would answer affirmatively. Each would form a reflective belief that the object has the property of falling to the earth when released. Where does this belief come from? Quite simply, without reason to believe otherwise, the nonreflective belief that physical objects require support or else plummet to the earth serves as a good first guess or default assumption for the formation of reflective beliefs. Our reflective mental capacities "read off" beliefs from our unconscious mental tools.[18] The outputs from unconscious mental tools (that is, nonreflective beliefs) serve as inputs for our reflective mental functions. Unless some salient competing or mitigating information challenges the nonreflective belief, it becomes adopted as a reflective belief.

In addition to the previously mentioned example, consider the following scenario. Suppose I observed a little girl go into a kitchen and leave with an apple. Then I see the child do it again and again. My ToM automatically tells me that people act in ways to satisfy desires, so a reasonable interpretation of this child's behaviors is that the child wants apples. My living-thing describer tells me that people and other animals eat when hungry. I get all this information nonreflectively. If the girl's behavior merited my attention (maybe I found it curious, maybe the apples were mine, or maybe I wanted an apple too) or someone directed my attention to the child by asking, "So why is that kid taking apples?" I might consciously form a belief about her desires. In many circumstances, this reflective belief would combine the nonreflective belief provided by my ToM—that she desires apples and is acting to satisfy that desire—with the nonreflective belief provided by my living-thing describer—that the girl is hungry. A reasonable and rapidly formed reflective belief would be that the girl is swiping apples because she is hungry.

Suppose, however, that I happened to know that earlier in the day the girl had enthusiastically commented that the horse outside would allow anyone to pet it when tempted by an apple. If I can consciously recollect this verbal information, then my reflective faculties may use this information together with any relevant nonreflective beliefs (that the girl desires apples or that the girl is hungry) to form a slightly different reflective belief. My ToM still says that the girl desires apples, but now I have two different possible reasons for the desire. Nonreflectively I believe she is hungry, but reflectively I have reason to believe she desires the apples to lure the horse. Dredging up some stored knowledge about little girls—that they rarely eat three whole apples in succession—I reflectively conclude that the girl wants the apples for the horse and that she is not in fact hungry. Note that though this reflective belief discounted one nonreflective belief regarding the girl's own hunger, the reflective belief strikes me as satisfying and plausible largely because it still meshes well with other underlying nonreflective beliefs: that girls act to satisfy desires and that horses desire food because they are animals and will act to satisfy their desires (even if that means being petted by a little girl).

Nonreflective Beliefs Make Reflective Beliefs More Plausible

As the previous scenario illustrates, nonreflective beliefs not only influence reflective beliefs by serving as default candidates for beliefs but also make reflective beliefs seem more plausible or more credible. When a reflective belief nicely matches what our nonconscious mental tools tell us through nonreflective beliefs, the reflective beliefs just seem more reasonable. Sometimes we say that such reflective beliefs seem right intuitively or that our intuitions tell us they are so. In fact, psychologists sometimes refer to our nonreflective beliefs as "intuitive beliefs or knowledge" and to our nonconscious mental tools as "intuitive reasoning systems." When someone else tells us about some idea or something that fits these intuitive mental tools, we tend to (reflectively) believe most readily. We find the idea intuitive.

Fitting with nonreflective beliefs may be a matter of either matching them (as in the previous example) or simply not violating them. For instance, compare the following two claims: 1) scientists have discovered things on another planet that can move from one place to another without passing through the space in between and 2) scientists have discovered things on another planet that can move from one place to another at speeds of 90,000 km/hr. Which claim seems more believable? For most people, the second claim is more plausible than the first because our object describer produces a nonreflective belief that when objects move from one place to another, they pass through the intervening space. Our object describer has no particular beliefs about how fast things move. Reflective beliefs might tell us that both claims are impossible. (In fact, the possibility of either claim is debated by physicists, with some reporting that particles have been shown to move from one place to another without passing through the intervening space.)

When we hear ideas that resonate with any beliefs we already have—nonreflective or otherwise—we are inclined to believe them, but nonreflective beliefs generated by intuitive mental tools remain special in this regard. Unlike preexisting beliefs that might arise through personal experience or education, the nonreflective beliefs generated by mental tools inhabit most all minds everywhere.

Nonreflective Beliefs Shape Memories and Experiences

A third and less direct way through which nonreflective beliefs shape reflective beliefs is by shaping experiences and memories for experiences. Sometimes people suppose that we experience events around us the way they are and remember things the way they really were as well. Not so, at least not exactly. Everything we experience must be processed and transformed through our nervous systems, including our brains. Some things get left out. Others get changed. Instead of thinking of our minds as blank slates or photographic film waiting to be impressed with whatever is "out there" or as a storage bin for whatever happens to come in, a more accurate metaphor for our minds is as a workshop that selectively brings in raw materials and then alters and combines those materials into new, useful units. Some of the primary tools used in the workshop of the mind are the nonconscious mental tools to which I have already referred.

With visual experiences, information about what is around us doesn't simply come in as it is. For instance, the eyes and brain receive information from light waves and organize it into colors, lines, edges, shapes, and objects. Many of the tools I call categorizers take this basic information and transform it yet again, breaking down the visual information into recognizable objects. That is, the categorizers form nonreflective beliefs about what is around us. The describers then add to the information from the categorizers to give our minds useful understandings about what is around us, what can be done with it, and what it might do to us. These, too, are nonreflective beliefs. By the time we get to the level of a conscious experience (which may be explicitly remembered or forgotten), the basic information about what is outside us in the environment has been drastically changed and augmented—transformed by nonreflective beliefs. Thus, when people reflectively try to evaluate claims to form beliefs and draw on experiences as evidence for or against those claims, the memories recalled as evidence actually include additions and changes contributed by nonreflective beliefs.

At times, the role of nonreflective beliefs in changing the evidence relied on for forming reflective beliefs may drastically impact the resulting reflective beliefs. To illustrate, when trying to form a reflective belief about how smart gerbils are, I am likely to draw, at least in part, on recollections of my experiences with gerbils and their behavior. I might think about how a gerbil I once observed seemed to display remarkable problem solving in moving bedding from one place to another in its overstuffed cheeks. I might recall how it seemed to contemplate its moves and consider its surroundings carefully. With these data, I might conclude that gerbils are fairly intelligent. Note, however, that all my memories were interpretive. The gerbil moved bedding from one place to another using its cheeks, and I interpreted it as the gerbil forming a desire, recognizing the usefulness of its own cheeks, and forming beliefs about how to use the holding ability of its cheeks to satisfy its desires. Whether this is what the gerbil actually did or whether it acted on brute instinct with none of these more sophisticated thoughts ever occurring is irrelevant to how my belief forms. I have no solid evidence to distinguish between these two options, but my intuitive mental tools provided me with nonreflective beliefs that color my memory of the animal's behavior. Similarly, what I remember as its contemplation might only be the consequence of my ToM attributing reflective abilities erroneously. Contemplation and vacant stupidity can look very similar from the outside. These nonreflective belief-tainted memories then serve as the corpus from which I form reflective beliefs.

Reflective beliefs—what we commonly talk about as beliefs—gain their plausibility from 1) their fit with nonreflective beliefs, 2) their fit with reflectively available evidence including memories and experiences (that might be colored by nonreflective beliefs), and 3) their fit with other reflective beliefs that were previously derived in the same way. Generally, the more ways in which a candidate belief is saliently supported, the more likely it becomes a reflective belief. The more mental systems or mental tools produce outputs consistent with the idea in question, the more likely it becomes a belief. Thus, a candidate belief that enjoys synchronicity with a large number of mental tools *and* that fits with various personal experiences *and* that makes sense of reported events or phenomena would likely become a reflective belief. Another way to express this principle is simply this: the more mental tools with which an idea fits, the more likely it is to become a belief. Belief in gods generally and God particularly is common because gods fit this principle quite well.

To clarify, I do not mean to imply that the bulk of reflective beliefs people hold arise through careful and thorough evaluation. The process by which reflective mental faculties decide to accept a belief often amounts to a crude heuristic— a quick-and-dirty strategy for making decisions. As mentioned previously, people rarely work through a logical and empirical proof for a claim. Rather, what I call "reflective" tools typically do their calculations rapidly. How many different nonreflective beliefs and available memories (for information or experiences) fit with the claim? If the number is large, then believe. Such a strategy often does the job efficiently, though sometimes it produces errors in judgment. Because our nonconscious mental tools that produce nonreflective beliefs are tuned to survival, we have reason to believe they tell us something close to the truth most of the time.[19]

Likewise, though potentially suffering from being nonrepresentative or idiosyncratic, our experiences function as a critical means for learning about the world around us. Consequently, the heuristic to believe easily those ideas that fit with a large number of nonreflective beliefs and experiences works reasonably well most the time.

I also do not mean to imply that the process through which we arrive at reflective beliefs is a transparent process and easily inspected. Though the consequence is "reflective" belief, the tabulation of nonreflective beliefs and the evaluation of this tabulation may remain largely unavailable to conscious consideration.

Even those beliefs for which we seem to have lots of reflectively accessible reasons often, in fact, have been arrived at nonreflectively, and the explicit reasons amount to justification after the fact and have little or nothing to do with the actual formation of the belief. For instance, though we may be able to make a list of reasons why we believe someone is a good friend, deciding that person would be a good friend was probably done with little or no conscious awareness or explicit rationale. Similarly, I might be able to explicitly marshal a weighty list of reasons for believing eating chicken is more appropriate than eating rabbit, but the complete story must include the fact that I was raised eating chicken and thinking of rabbits as pets. Consequently, I nonreflectively categorize rabbits as pets and not as livestock, thereby weakening my desire to eat rabbits. Any explicit justifications for this belief about the edibility of chickens relative to rabbits probably amount to rationalization of a nonconscious aversion to eating a pet.

In a religious context, many believers can give numerous explicit reasons why they believe in God, but the process of arriving at this belief probably involved few, if any, of these explicit reasons and even then only in part. As the rest of this book shows, belief in God arises through a host of reasons that typically escape reflective notice.

Why Do We Believe?

To summarize, I see what we commonly call "beliefs" as constituting a subset of beliefs I term *reflective*. These reflective beliefs commonly (but not exclusively) arise directly or indirectly from a second group of beliefs called *nonreflective*. Nonconscious, intuitive mental tools routinely and perpetually spill out nonreflective beliefs as they attempt to organize and make useful information about the world around us. These rapidly generated nonreflective beliefs not only help us solve problems negotiating our environment without taxing conscious mental resources but also serve as our first and best guess for constructing reflective beliefs.

When placed in a situation that demands a reflective belief, our conscious mental faculties begin by "reading off" relevant nonreflective beliefs. When no obvious reason presents itself to discard the nonreflective belief, we accept it as our reflective belief. In situations in which the candidate belief in question cannot be merely read off, nonreflective beliefs still weigh in to influence the reflective judgment. Beliefs that appear consistent with or that resonate with nonreflective beliefs give existential satisfaction, an intuitiveness. Nonreflective beliefs also serve as the glasses through which we view experiences and recall memories that might be brought to the reflective table as evidence for a particular belief.

Thus, at least when considering the ordinary beliefs of people in everyday settings (as opposed to academic or analytical settings), much of belief can be accounted for without appealing to any special reasoning. Whether a belief arose through personal experience versus secondhand account, through an authoritative source, through the senses, or through logical argumentation remains largely irrelevant at this level. Beliefs that considerably jibe with the outputs of the nonconscious mental tools that people have all over the world will be more likely to be embraced and to spread within and across cultures.

It might be helpful to think of the process in terms of a chairperson trying to determine the consensus opinion of a group of people, whether to agree with a proposition or to reject it. Each individual in the group has a belief about whether the proposition is true or false, but these beliefs vary in strength. When the chairperson, who represents the reflective mind, asks what everyone thinks, the chair gets some "definite yes" votes, some "well I guess so" votes, some "probably not" votes, some "no way" votes, and some abstentions. Think of these votes as the nonreflective beliefs registered by various mental tools. Both the strength of the commitments and the valence (positive or negative) matter to the chair in trying to reach a group decision.[20] Similarly, the various mental tools provide belief, antibelief, or no position at all, and these nonreflective beliefs may range in strength. The strength of the nonreflective beliefs are determined in part by built-in biases of the mental tools and in part by how frequently such beliefs receive exercise. Those beliefs that see the most activity, however, will tend to be those naturally supported by biases of the mental tools in the first place. The rest of this book argues that many theological beliefs, such as believing in God, are just these types of beliefs that are greatly supported by intuitive mental tools.

Notes

1. Dan Sperber (1997) makes a similar distinction, using the terms "intuitive beliefs" and "reflective beliefs."

2. I realize some philosophers may wince at the way I use "belief"—especially "nonreflective beliefs"—but remember that my business here is to show why people go about holding the beliefs they hold (whether or not they know they hold them) and not whether they *should* hold these beliefs. "Nonreflective beliefs" may more closely approach what philosophers sometimes call "knowledge." I include among nonreflective beliefs both tacit knowledge that just has not necessarily been made explicit (such as that a wooden floor

would support human weight) and those implicit expectations we have of things that apply to novel situations and things (such as that all objects require support or else fall to the earth). I have chosen not to use the term "knowledge" because it obscures some important relationships and differences between reflective and nonreflective beliefs.

3. Anthropologist John Tooby and psychologist Leda Cosmides (Cosmides, Tooby, & Barkow, 1992; Tooby & Cosmides, 1992) argue similarly that the mind might be thought of as akin to a Swiss Army knife, having many specialized tools. For an accessible overview of the mind's specialized functions, I recommend Steven Pinker's *How the Mind Works* (1997).

4. The names for the different tools are mine with the exception of the Theory of Mind (ToM) device. Evidence for the existence of these specialized tools comes primarily from experimental work in cognitive developmental psychology. Two volumes that provide thorough introductions to this area of research are *Mapping the Mind: Domain Specificity in Cognition and Culture* (Hirschfeld & Gelman, 1994) and the more rigorous but less accessible *Causal Cognition: A Multidisciplinary Debate* (Sperber, Premack, & Premack, 1995).

5. For this fascinating line of research on babies' ability to imitate facial expressions, see works by Meltzoff and Moore (1983, 1989, 1992, 1994).

6. Some disagreement exists over whether the same mental device is used for identifying an object and then for generating descriptions and other inferences about it. It may be that in many cases the two functions are subserved by the same structures in the brain.

7. Spelke (1991); Spelke, Phillips, and Woodward (1995); Spelke and Van de Walle (1993).

8. Keil (1989, 1992, 1994, 1995); Simons and Keil (1995).

9. For a recent review of research in the theory of mind area, see Wellman, Cross, and Watson (2001).

10. Cosmides (1989) and Cosmides and Tooby (1989) have championed the existence of such a mental tool using evolutionary, cross-cultural, and experimental observations.

11. Henrich and Gil-White (2001).

12. See Katz (2000) for evolutionary perspectives and Turiel (1998) for a child developmental perspective.

13. Bloom (1998); Gelman, Durgin, and Kaufman (1995); Spelke et al. (1995).

14. For example, consider Clifford and Walster (1973) and Dion (1972). Myers (1990) accessibly describes the physical attractiveness stereotype and some of the supporting evidence that, sometimes quite unaware, people view those who are physically attractive as possessing numerous desirable traits. As Myers sums up, "Added together, the findings point to a *physical-attractiveness stereotype:* What is beautiful is good" (p. 421; emphasis in the original).

15. Work by M. Banaji and others (Banaji & Bhaskar, 2000; Banaji & Greenwald, 1994) shows, using carefully designed computer tasks, that people who disavow any racist attitudes may show racist biases in their automatic abilities to connect ideas. For instance, when asked to sort words in a time-pressured task, American adults (of all races) tend to more rapidly sort negative-valence words with African American faces than with white faces. For demonstrations and additional details of these effects, see http://implicit.harvard.edu/implicit.

16. Sometimes nonreflective or intuitive cognition also fills in the blanks that theology leaves. For example, in Christianity exactly what sorts of things might be intuitively more sensible to pray for seems to be guided by completely nontheological activities of mental tools (Barrett, 2001).

17. Barrett (1998); Barrett and Keil (1996); Barrett and Van Orman (1996). See Barrett (1999) for a review and discussion of implications for the study of religious concepts. Tremlin (2002) has developed these ideas even further to account for recurrent patterns of religious thought and development.

18. Anthropologist and psychologist Pascal Boyer (2001) makes a similar observation in chapter 9 of his book *Religion Explained: The Evolutionary Origins of Religious Development.*

19. Though some cognitive scientists assume that because our brains and their functions have been "designed" by natural selection we can trust them to tell us the truth, such an assumption is epistemologically dubious. Just because we can successfully survive and reproduce in no way ensures that our minds as a whole tell us the truth about anything—especially when it comes to sophisticated thinking. Being able to understand quantum physics is something our minds can do, but it is far from obvious that the prerequisite capacities were *necessary* for survival in our prehistoric past. Indeed, some (perhaps most) of us do not have the mental capacities for understanding the truth claims in quantum physics or simpler scientific truths, but that doesn't impede our ability to survive and reproduce. Similarly, plenty of organisms survive and reproduce without their simpler nervous systems producing much that we should feel comfortable calling "truth." Further, psychologists have proven repeatedly that our minds are *not* naturally tuned to represent truth. Even in basic perception, we get things wrong all the time by selectively attending to and distorting information as it comes in. What a completely naturalistic view of the human mind may safely embrace is merely that our minds were good for survival *in the past.*

20. I talk throughout this book as if the mind stores and evaluates propositions and sometimes as if the mind is a symbolic processor. I find this a convenient way to make sense of the functions of the mind but am not advocating that propositions or symbols literally find residence in the brain itself. My story could be retold in a comparable manner by referring to the functional outcomes of connectionist systems.

Where Do Beliefs in Gods Come From? Religious Concepts as Minimally Counterintuitive

BELIEF IN GODS requires no special parts of the brain. Belief in gods requires no special mystical experiences, though it may be aided by such experiences. Belief in gods requires no coercion or brainwashing or special persuasive techniques. Rather, belief in gods arises because of the natural functioning of completely normal mental tools working in common natural and social contexts.

In chapter 1, I explained that the more mental tools with which an idea fits, the more likely it is to become a (reflective) belief. With this principle in hand, I now turn to the origins of belief in gods. I argue that belief in gods comes about through the same mental processes as any other beliefs, using the same mental tools. Belief in gods is common precisely because such beliefs resonate with and receive support from a large number of mental tools. To begin, I describe why people find concepts of gods and other superhuman and nonnatural beings attention demanding and memorable because of how minds represent their conceptual structure. Then, in chapters 3 and 4, I detail a number of additional specific mental tools that make concepts of gods likely to be embraced.[1]

By "gods," I mean broadly any number of superhuman beings in whose existence at least a single group of people believe and who behave on the basis of these beliefs. Under this definition, I do not discriminate between ghosts, demons, chimeras (such as centaurs or satyrs), or the supreme gods of religions. Even space aliens may count. They qualify as "gods," for my purposes, as long as people's activity in some way is modified by these beliefs and they are not merely people with ordinary properties of people—a point I develop in this chapter.

Minimally Counterintuitive Concepts

Cognitive anthropologist and psychologist Pascal Boyer observed that religious concepts, including concepts of gods, ghosts, and spirits, may be counted within a large class of concepts I have termed "minimally counterintuitive" (MCI) concepts.[2] These MCIs may be characterized as meeting most of the assumptions that describers and categorizers generate—thus being easy to understand, remember, and believe—but as violating just enough of these assumptions to be attention demanding and to have an unusually captivating ability to assist in the explanation of certain experiences. These MCIs commonly occupy important roles in mythologies, legends, folktales, religious writings, and stories of peoples all over the world.[3]

Create an MCI in the following way. First, take an ordinary concept, such as "tree," "shoe," or "dog," that meets all of the naturally occurring assumptions of our categorizers and describers. Then *violate* one of the assumptions. For instance, as a bounded physical object, a tree activates the nonreflective beliefs governing physical objects, including being visible. So make the tree invisible (otherwise a perfectly good tree), and you have an MCI. Similarly, an MCI may be made by *transferring* an assumption from another category of things. A shoe, as an artifact (human-made thing), is not assumed to grow or develop. These assumptions deal with living things. Hence, a shoe that grows old and dies would be an MCI, whereas a dog that grows old and dies is ordinary. Constructing MCIs merely consists of either violating a property (or a small number of properties) nonreflectively assumed by categorizers and describers or transferring a property (or a small number of properties) from a different category of things that is nonreflectively assumed for the other category.

Because what qualifies a concept as MCI is determined by the nonreflective beliefs of categorizers and describers and because categorizers and describers operate essentially the same way in all people everywhere, what is MCI in one culture is MCI in any other culture. A person who can walk through walls is MCI anywhere. A rock that talks is MCI anywhere. This independence from cultural relativism enables identification as an MCI to be a valuable tool in making pan-cultural predictions and explanations.

Note that being MCI doesn't necessarily (though often does) mean that the concept is nonnatural or untrue. Arguably, plants that eat animals are MCI, yet several species of plants (such as Venus's-flytraps) do so. Likewise, an MCI concept is not the same as an unusual or bizarre concept. I may encounter animal-eating plants regularly but never experience a plant named George. A plant named George may be unusual or bizarre but certainly is not MCI. A plant that eats animals is MCI but may not necessarily be unusual or bizarre. What amounts to a bizarre concept *varies* by individual experiences and cultural factors, whereas whether a concept is MCI does not.

MCIs, then, constitute a special group of concepts—concepts that largely match intuitive assumptions about their own group of things but have a small number of tweaks that make them particularly interesting and memorable. Because they are more interesting and memorable, they are more likely to be passed on from person to person. Because they readily spread from person to person, MCIs are likely to become cultural (that is, widely shared) concepts.

Of course, it is possible to transfer or violate multiple properties and create concepts that do not qualify as *minimally* counterintuitive. For instance, a dog that was made in a factory, gives birth to chickens, can talk to people, is invisible, can read minds, can walk through walls, and can never die would be counterintuitive. But such a dog would be far from *minimally* counterintuitive. Adding violation after violation and transfer after transfer confuses the categorizers and describers to such a degree that these concepts become cumbersome and difficult to remember or make sense of. What we are left with is a laundry list of features. People do not easily remember such massively counterintuitive concepts, so it is not surprising that they do not frequently appear in folktales or mythologies or even modern science-fiction novels.

Another breed of difficult counterintuitive concepts consists of those that both transfer a property and violate its assumptions. For instance, a shoe that can hear you talking would be MCI. The property of hearing has been transferred from people (or animals) to an artifact. A person who can hear everything would be MCI because limitations on ability to hear have been violated. A shoe that can hear everything, however, would be a more problematic counterintuitive because the transferred property (hearing) has been violated (no limitations on hearing). Such concepts, like the maximally counterintuitives, also give people great difficulties in remembering and understanding and consequently do not spread well. These concepts do not frequently occur as religious or other cultural concepts. Though people sometimes talk about and believe in statues (artifacts) that can hear prayers, these people do not often believe that the statues can hear you anywhere. In fact, people typically speak to these statues from a distance similar to the distance they would use in talking to ordinary people.[4]

Many religious concepts clearly fall into the category of MCI. For instance, ancestor spirits that play a major role in many local religions around the world may be characterized as concepts of people—with all the assumed, nonreflective beliefs about people—plus a couple of counterintuitive features. These counterintuitive features amount to a simple negation of physical object assumptions of people, for example, being tangible and visible. The ancestor spirits amount to ordinary people without physical bodies. Because believers understand them as people, they can easily and efficiently reason about their beliefs, desires, motivations, and behaviors. Events, such as the death of a prize animal, may be attributed to the vengeful action of an ancestor because of some transgression. All this is very sensible and intuitive. The mental tools (especially the Theory of Mind) that handle such matters proceed seamlessly. However, because ancestor spirits have no physical bodies, the notion of them also creates interest and speculation that might not take place when reasoning about ordinary people. Where might they be? Did they see the sin I committed yesterday? Are they pleased with us? Events may be attributed to them that could not be credited to people; had a person done it, we would have seen it. Similarly, gods, ghosts, demons, angels, witches, shamans, oracles, prophets, and many other members of religious casts of characters appear to meet a sort of optimum of being largely intuitive but having enough counterintuitive features that make them memorable, attention demanding, and able to be used to explain and predict events and phenomena. If they were too hard to conceptualize, people might not be able to make sense of them in real time to solve problems, tell stories, or understand the implications of them for their own behavior. If they were too intuitive, they would gather so little attention that they would soon be forgotten.

MCI Concepts That Fail to Spread

Though Boyer and others have experimentally and cross-culturally shown MCIs to be memorable and more likely to be passed on faithfully than either ordinary concepts or bizarre ones,[5] MCIs do not outnumber the other two classes of concepts in either oral or written communication. Naturally, ordinary, intuitive concepts are most numerous. Perhaps the simplest reason is that most things with which we interact fall into the category of intuitive concepts. Though MCIs do exist in the world, intuitive things vastly outnumber them. Hence, intuitive concepts become the backdrop for talk about MCIs.

A second reason for the relative rarity of MCIs compared to intuitive concepts has to do with our earlier discussion of nonreflective and reflective concepts sometimes contradicting each other. In chapter 1, I explained that in contexts requiring the rapid handling and processing of complicated concepts (those not well grounded in nonreflective beliefs, such as many theological ones), these reflective concepts lose many (if not all) of their features *not* supported by nonreflective beliefs. That is, counterintuitive concepts degrade into intuitive ones. Consequently, even if one had an enormous repertoire of MCI concepts, when trying to use many at once in a single narrative, for instance, many would be degraded into intuitive versions. This degradation is a necessary consequence of limitations on how much novel (that is, not intuitive) information our minds can retain and use at one time.

A third reason for MCIs remaining relatively uncommon implicates some additional factors that help explain the commonness of belief in gods. Many different MCIs are possible and memorable, but not all appear frequently in cultural materials or communication. Though an invisible tree is just as much an MCI as a listening tree, ethnographers tell us that things like trees and rocks that listen appear much more commonly in belief systems—and even folktales that may not be believed—than invisible objects that are otherwise ordinary. Similarly, animals made in factories are MCI, but animals that can speak appear in mythologies, tales, and religions. So what is the difference between these MCIs?

Imagine you heard about a rock that vanished every time someone looked at it. Though such a thing would be MCI—having the two physical violations of being invisible and changing its physical properties when not directly contacted—the vanishing rock would not likely become part of any religious system or even part of folklore. Indeed, while stories of animals with the minds of people, accounts of artifacts coming to life, and many other types of MCIs abound, you would be hard-pressed to find stories about objects that vanish when you looked at them. These MCIs simply do a poor job of generating additional inferences or explanations. Thus, they generate little interest and aren't worth talking about.[6] So what if there is a rock that vanishes whenever anyone looks at it? What follows from that? Similarly, imagine a person who has absolutely no desires. MCI? Sure. Worth thinking about? Not really. Or a tree that does not grow or die. MCI? You bet. Interesting? Not to me.

These examples show that being MCI is not enough for an idea to become a well-spread cultural idea or belief, let alone a religious idea or belief. Something else is needed. Some other factor or factors must make the concepts that become the stuff of religion mentally contagious.

Successful MCI Concepts

For MCIs to successfully compete for space in human minds and thus become "cultural," they must have the potential to explain, to predict, or to generate interesting stories surrounding them. In short, MCIs must have good *inferential potential*. Rocks that disappear when looked at or invisible trees or people who have no desires and do absolutely nothing have little inferential potential. It would be hard to build stories or accounts around such inferentially impoverished MCIs. They don't make sense of things that have happened or might happen to us. They don't help explain the way things are. They don't *activate* many other mental tools or reasoning.

Concepts that are most likely to have strong inferential potential, activating large numbers of mental tools and exciting reasoning, are those that qualify as intentional agents. The MCIs that folktales, mythologies, and stories feature have minds that drive their behaviors. Whether they are listening trees, talking animals, or cunning computers, all qualify as *agents*—beings that do not merely respond mechanistically to the world around them but also act on the world because of internal (mental) states. Similarly, religions do not center on such things as sticks that people can use to move objects (we would call that magic or technology, not religion) or sofas that exist only during full moons but rather on people with superpowers, statues that can answer requests, or disembodied minds that can act on us and the world. The most central concepts in religions are related to agents.

Agents have tremendous inferential potential. Agents can cause things to happen, not only be caused. We can explain why things are so by appealing to agents. We can anticipate what an agent might do. We can't anticipate what a rock might do, only what might be done to it. Not surprisingly, then, from space aliens to humanlike animals to cartoon characters to God, intentional agents are the MCIs that people tell stories about, remember, and tell to others.

First Candidates for Religious Beliefs: MCIs That People Believe

Note, however, that not all MCIs—even if they are agents—gain the status of "religious." To become part of religious thought, the existence of these MCI agents must be believed. As explained in chapter 1, reflective belief in concepts typically requires a substantial overlap with nonreflective beliefs. At first glance, it seems that MCIs, by definition, would be largely incredible. After all, they explicitly *violate* nonreflective beliefs. How then might MCIs be believable?

The principle I introduced in chapter 1 was that the more mental tools with which an idea fits, the more likely it is to become a belief. MCIs match mental tools' outputs—nonreflective beliefs—very well but include a small number of explicit violations, weakening their overall plausibility. However, some MCIs exchange a violation of intuitive assumptions for a stronger fit with other mental tools and experiences. Let's begin with a simple example: the Venus's-flytrap. The notion of a plant that moves suddenly to eat animals but otherwise is a perfectly good plant amounts to a MCI. A priori, it would seem somewhat less plausible than a plant that grows only five inches tall but otherwise is a perfectly good plant. However, if I happen to see a Venus's-flytrap close its modified leaf on an ant or fly, my mental tools that causally record what I just saw tell me that the most sensible interpretation of the event is that the plant eats animals (and not that it accidentally folded a leaf in half at the same time the leaf was contacted by an insect). As counterintuitive as it may be—violating the nonpredator assumption of plants—more mental tools agree with the claim that the Venus's-flytrap preys on insects than disagree with that conclusion. Thus, on balance, the MCI reflective belief about Venus's-flytraps seems plausible, and I believe it.

Similarly, when considering religious beliefs or other cultural beliefs that may be characterized as MCI, those that make a "profitable exchange"—trading an intuitive property or two for better activation and fit with other mental tools—will be plausible and believed. For instance, around a large citrus ranch in California, all the locals know about the Chivo Man who roams the "haunted dairy." Presumed by some to have been invented a generation ago by a mother trying to keep her children away from crumbling buildings, the story of the elusive and dangerous part-goat Chivo Man is now part of local cultural knowledge and regarded by many as true.[7] Rarely does anyone actually report an encounter with the Chivo Man, and the notion of a part human, part goat creature certainly violates intuitive assumptions about animals being one and only one species. Why then might the Chivo Man be not only well spread but actually believed in by some? Though the details of this example might require fuller exploration by an ethnographer, my contention is that the Chivo Man concept (for at least those who believe) has exchanged a violation of one or two intuitive assumptions for a better fit with other mental tools. Suppose that a young man named Steve had heard the story of the Chivo Man told with great conviction by a trustworthy person with nothing obvious to gain from others believing the story. At a later time, Steve happened to be passing by the crumbling haunted dairy and was nearly struck by falling shingles, even though the day was windless. Startled by the incident, he searched for who or what had caused the shingles to fall. But he saw no one. Puzzled, he cautiously continued past the ruins, stepping past what looked like goat droppings. Strange—he had never heard of any goats being grazed here, nor were there any around. Then he remembered the story of the Chivo Man.

Would Steve believe in the Chivo Man? Automatically, his reflective mental systems would "read off" the outputs of other systems. On one side of the plausibility ledger, Steve's living-thing describer says the Chivo Man does not fit assumptions. On the other side, consider the following:

- His object describer reports that shingles don't just fall on their own, and his agency detection device registers a strong likelihood that someone had caused shingles to fall on him.
- His store of knowledge relevant to goats sends an affirmative regarding the droppings, but his memory for the setting offers no memory of actual goats.
- His Theory of Mind reasons that if he was assaulted, someone desired to harm him, and his knowledge of territorialism offers trespassing as a candidate transgression worthy of retaliation.
- His knowledge that people rarely come to the haunted dairy and that it inexplicably remains in ruins finds a satisfying cause in the presence of a hostile guardian.
- His social exchange regulator tells him that the woman from whom he heard the story was trustworthy.

Given these inputs, the faculties determining reflective beliefs may prompt him, at least tentatively, to hold a belief in the Chivo Man. After all, many mental tools either independently or in coordination seem to support the plausibility of the Chivo Man for Steve. Not all people would reason in exactly the same way. The point of the Chivo Man illustration is not to convince you that one *should* believe in the Chivo Man or that Steve's belief in the Chivo Man is *justified*. The Chivo Man story shows only *how* someone might come to believe in an MCI concept, that is, what the process might be.

Note again that this is mostly an unconscious process. Though we are now talking about reflective beliefs, the determination of plausibility is nonreflective. Reflective determination of plausibility is something that people rarely engage in unless they are formally trained to do so by scholars. Rather, they just "feel" that the belief is sensible. Unless one is trained in logic or empirical reasoning, even when required to offer justification, whatever "pops into mind" first may seem a good enough justification. This "popping into mind" typically amounts to nothing more than a fragmentary reiteration of the nonreflective plausibility determination. The "reasons" for belief suggested earlier in this chapter certainly don't amount to any kind of argument for belief and may seem biased to attend to the evidence that supports belief instead of challenging belief. People find reasons for a belief much more rapidly and with greater ease than they find reasons against a belief. Indeed, much of the training in the social and natural sciences is teaching skepticism and how to find alternative explanations. It does not come easily.

I used an example of a MCI agent (Chivo Man) because it is MCI agents that most often activate a broad range of mental tools and hence seem plausible and become believed. As fundamentally social beings, we have a huge number of experiences interacting with others. To accommodate these social interactions, our minds develop a vast array of mental tools and "social intelligences." Agent concepts (including MCIs) have the potential to trigger many of these social mental tools (mostly from the group I called facilitators in chapter 1), enhancing their potential credibility. Contrast agent concepts with vanishing rocks. At best, the suggestion of a vanishing rock could account for someone tripping on what looks like smooth ground and excite some inferences about how such a rock might be used as a tool. On the plausibility ledger, the violation of physical expectations (vanishing when looked at) substantially outweighs any ability to prompt other mental tools to generate congruent nonreflective beliefs. That the rock vanishes does not drive inferences or enhance plausibility any better than the rock being brown would. The vanishing rock cannot begin to support inferences regarding morality in social interaction, why trouble befalls some people, how the rains come, why the crops succeed or fail, or what happens to the dead. MCI agents can.

Not So *Minimally* Counterintuitive Concepts

Though many religious concepts have a small number of counterintuitive properties that enhance their inferential potential, some religious ideas seem far from *minimally* counterintuitive. Common concepts of God, for instance, appear to be massively counterintuitive, including such properties as being immortal, all-knowing, all-powerful, nontemporal, nonspatial, a trinity, and so forth. As I will show in chapter 6, some of these divine properties may not be as counterintuitive as they first seem; nevertheless, some theological beliefs, more typically held by clergy and theologians than regular folk, do have a large number of counterintuitive features and do not fit the MCI label.

The spread of counterintuitive concepts may be aided by a couple of different factors. Religious events may be used to develop and make more sophisticated religious beliefs. If a person believes in an MCI god, through rigorous theological instruction they may be led to accept additional counterintuitive properties of the god. Building on an MCI foundation, greater deviations from nonreflective beliefs may gradually be acquired through much explicit repetition and argumentation that persuasively connects these fancier ideas with the more intuitive ones already in place. However, note that (as discussed in chapter 1) too many counterintuitive properties may not easily be used in normal day-to-day reasoning about gods. Consequently, though people may claim to believe in complex theological ideas, the utility of such beliefs for generating inferences and motivating actions may remain low.

In addition to explicit and repetitive instruction, more complex religious beliefs may be formed because of the contextual nature of concepts. For simplicity's sake, I discussed counterintuitive properties as if concepts are single, context-free, encapsulated units. A concept with only a small number of counterintuitive properties that increase the concept's inferential potential will more readily spread and be believed. More precisely, a concept with only a small number of counterintuitive properties that increase the concept's inferential potential *in any given transmissive context* will more readily spread and be believed. To illustrate, if in one context God is described much like any other agent but as having the property of being outside time (nontemporal), such a concept would qualify as MCI. In another context, God might be characterized as existing as a trinity but with each person of the trinity having fairly ordinary properties otherwise. This concept of God would likewise be MCI. Independently, each of these concepts of God might be readily adopted through the mechanisms described previously. Then, because of a common label ("God"), these two concepts could be seamlessly fused. Though putting both properties in the same context could make "God" too complex to be considered MCI and thus difficult to transmit and believe, people may reflectively affirm such a complex concept when it is acquired cumulatively through diverse contexts.

Taking Stock so Far

In chapter 1, I argued that most beliefs people hold arise from a collection of non-conscious mental tools automatically generating assumptions about the way things are in the world. These nonreflective beliefs often become the basis for the creation of reflective beliefs. The credibility of reflective beliefs is (nonreflectively) enhanced by close matches with the output of many different mental tools. The more mental tools (including those that store memories of experiences and communications) agree with the possibility that something is true, the more likely that idea becomes a reflectively embraced belief.

In this chapter, I have elaborated the argument to include MCIs—concepts that do violate a small number of assumptions generated by the mental tools called categorizers and describers. These MCIs may be quite memorable and easy to transmit to others and may also be believable—provided that the violations they make enable them to activate a broader range of mental tools in their support than would be possible without the violations. MCI agents typically fit this description better than other MCIs. Consequently, it is MCI agents that become believed and become part of religious systems. Theologians and religious leaders cannot simply teach any ideas they want and expect those ideas to be remembered, spread, and believed; rather, the way human minds operate gradually selects only those with the best fit to become widespread.

Notes

1. I discuss "God" more specifically in chapters 6 and 7.

2. I introduced this term in Barrett (2000), but the theoretical insights behind the notion should be credited to Boyer.

3. For Boyer's treatment of these widespread cultural concepts, see Boyer (1993, 1994, 1995, 1996, 1998, 2000, 2001, especially chapters 1 and 2), and Boyer and Walker (2000).

4. For instance, observe the distance from which Roman Catholics address images of saints.

5. For experimental evidence supporting these claims, see Barrett and Nyhof (2001). Boyer and Ramble (2001) provide corroborating cross-cultural data.

6. Sperber and Wilson (1995) comparably argue that in communicative settings, human minds seek out the most information for attentional investment. This ratio of inferential potential per conceptual investment may be termed "relevance."

7. The Chivo Man concept is not purely local but may be found in parts of Mexico as well. Thus, the local "invention" of a Chivo Man inhabiting the haunted dairy may more accurately amount to the importation of a concept acquired elsewhere. For the purposes of illustration, however, I will speak of just the one Chivo Man.

Where Do Beliefs in Gods Come From? Finding Agents Everywhere

3

THE INFERENTIAL POTENTIAL and relative plausibility of minimally counterintuitive (MCI) concepts are not the only factors contributing to their
frequency in cultural materials or their prominence in religious systems.
Part of the reason people believe in gods, ghosts, and goblins also comes from the
way in which our minds, particularly our agency detection device (ADD) functions. Our ADD suffers from some hyperactivity, making it prone to find agents
around us, including supernatural ones, given fairly modest evidence of their presence. This tendency encourages the generation and spread of god concepts and
other religious concepts.

Anthropologist Stewart Guthrie revived and refined the theory that religion
amounts to systematized "anthropomorphism"—the making of the cosmos in the
image of people.[1] Part of this theory is an important observation that is supported
by numerous experimental studies with adults and children as well as anthropological data. Guthrie astutely noted that people seem to have a strong bias to interpret
ambiguous evidence as caused by or being an agent. When hearing a bump in the
night, our first impulse is to wonder *who* caused the noise and not *what* caused the
noise. As other agents (such as humans and animals) present both our most important resources for survival and reproduction and our greatest threats, Guthrie
argues that such a perceptual bias would bestow survival advantages and thus, from
an evolutionary perspective, would be expected. We constantly scan our environment for the presence of other people and nonhuman agents. If you bet that something is an agent and it isn't, not much is lost. But if you bet that something is not
an agent and it turns out to be one, you could be lunch.

The mental tool responsible for the nonreflective detection of agency in the
environment is the ADD. As Guthrie has suggested, the ADD may be a little

hyperactive or hypersensitive to detecting agency. To emphasize this point, I sometimes refer to the mental tool as HADD—the hypersensitive agent detection device.[2]

HADD and Objects as Agents

Experimental work with adults and infants suggests that objects bearing little resemblance to people or even animals may be identified as agents.[3] The way people treat computers is a fine case in point. But even colored dots on a video display may do the trick and get HADD identifying them as agents and passing on this identification to the Theory of Mind (ToM) that then reasons about the dots as thinking, feeling beings. It seems that all that is needed for HADD to identify something as an agent is for the object to move itself (or in some other way act) in a way that suggests a goal for its action. In a classic study replicated numerous times, adults observed a film of geometric shapes moving in and around a broken square. At the conclusion of the film, observers recounted what they had seen. Strikingly, they described the geometric shapes as having mental states, such as beliefs and desires, and even personalities and sometimes genders.[4] These rich attributions of agency were sparked by contingent movement between two geometric shapes. Arguably, ignoring resemblance to known agents and risking false detection could have provided human ancestors with a selective advantage, detecting partially hidden, camouflaged, or disguised agents in the environment and only occasionally misidentifying wind-blown tree branches as agents. Such mistaken agent detection could quickly be turned off, minimizing costs of the error.

Though a nonreflective and crude system for finding agency, HADD, in working with other mental tools, may be sophisticated enough to reduce detection errors by paying attention to the known agents in the environment. Though people may treat geometric shapes as having beliefs, desires, and temperaments when they appear to move in a noninertial manner toward a goal, such movement information need not trigger such an identification. For instance, in one study using ball bearings made to move with hidden magnets, adults in one condition tended to make agent attributions to the ball bearings: they triggered HADD by moving in a way inconsistent with nonreflective beliefs governing simple physical objects. Nevertheless, in a second condition in which the adults indirectly controlled when the marbles moved (but not how they moved), they did not attribute agency. Why not? HADD appears to register noninertial, goal-directed movement as caused by an agent and then searches for a candidate agent. If a person or other known agent clearly accounts for the action, the object that moves need not be identified as an agent. If no such known agent is responsible for the movement, the object itself becomes a prime candidate for agency. Thus, we treat remote-control toys, cars, and computers as agents only when they "act" in a way that challenges our own agency (or the agency of another person).[5]

My examples, as well as the bulk of experimental work in the area, focuses on self-propelled movement; however, other actions triggered without physical contact could qualify as self-propelled and purposeful "movement" for HADD. So, if an object vocalizes without being physically contacted in what appears to be a purposeful reaction to events around it, HADD might identify the object as an agent. Computers don't move, but they do present information, create visual displays, or otherwise function in manners that may appear unrelated to any strictly mechanistic causation. Thus, we frequently attribute them agency and reason about them as such, especially when they act in ways seemingly unrelated to our own agency.

To summarize, when HADD perceives an object violating the intuitive assumptions for the movement of ordinary physical objects (such as moving on noninertial paths, changing direction inexplicably, or launching itself from a standstill) and the object seems to be moving in a goal-directed manner, HADD detects agency. Gathering information from other mental tools, HADD searches for any known agents that might account for the self-propelled movement. Finding none, HADD assumes that the object itself is an agent. Until information arrives to say otherwise, HADD registers a nonreflective belief that the object is an agent, triggering ToM to describe the object's activity in terms of beliefs, desires, and other mental states.

Sometimes HADD's tendency to attach agency to objects contributes to the formation of religious concepts. The most straightforward manner is in identifying some ambiguous thing, such as a wispy form, as an intentional agent—a ghost or spirit. With the assistance of face detectors and other tools sensitive to human forms, occasionally people see what appear to be humanlike figures. HADD may then discover evidence that these figures don't just physically resemble humans but are, indeed, thinking, feeling beings. Whether the sighting is an illusion or not, if the right information is fed to these mental tools, the outcome is a nonreflective belief in a ghost or spirit. Without sufficient reflective defenses, this nonreflective belief will become a reflective one.

HADD's tendency to find agency in objects contributes to the formation of religious concepts in a second manner. Often the objects that HADD registers as being agents are known objects. Unlike in the case of spirits, HADD may suggest that known nonagents are exhibiting agency. A storm cloud might have destroyed one and only one home in a village with hail and lightning. Under some conditions, HADD might register the cloud as an agent acting purposefully. But a cloud is not an agent. As in the case of the ball-bearing experiment, though HADD may have detected an object behaving like an agent, a more salient candidate may be attributed responsibility for the action in question. For instance, if villagers believe a certain god controls the weather, the storm cloud's apparent agency might be directed by that god against the reprobate individual. In these cases, HADD encourages belief in already known superhuman agents.

HADD and Identifying Events as the Result of Superhuman Agency

Consider the following event. A coworker of my wife once performed maintenance tasks on a farm. One day, Doug was working in a grain silo when leaked propane exploded. The first explosion rushed all around him and out the second-level windows high above him. Stunned by not being harmed by the blast, he tried to get out the door, only to discover that the explosion had jammed the doors. Knowing that a second, larger explosion was coming and he had no way out, Doug muttered hopelessly, "Take me home, Lord." He distinctly heard a voice say, "Not yet," and then felt some invisible hands lift him a dozen feet in the air and out of a second-story window, then safely to the ground below. Once he landed outside the silo, a safe distance away, the silo and attached barn exploded into rubble. He stumbled to the farm office, where coworkers took him to the hospital. At the hospital, Doug told the doctor that God sent angels to save him. The dumbfounded doctor reluctantly agreed it was a possibility given that the amount of propane gas in the man's lungs should have been fatal, yet he was not only alive but also conscious and talking. Doug, the doctor, and all staff of the farm believed this event to be caused by supernatural agency. In each of their minds, HADD played a major role in forming this belief.

Though receiving far less experimental attention, HADD also seems quite prone to detect agency that is not physically present in the form of an object. We don't always see important agents in our environment, only the consequences of their behaviors. Though our ability to reason readily about nonpresent agents facilitates thinking about ghosts and gods, as we will see, thinking about people who are not here right now and about hypothetical people who may or may not exist likewise requires such an ability. Thus, HADD does not require an object acting to be present in order to detect agency.

As when detecting what is thought to be an agent, when HADD detects agency, it activates ToM and other relevant mental tools to begin reasoning through how and why an agent might have acted. When we attend to an event that has no obvious mechanistic or biological cause (as understood by the object describer and the living-thing describer), HADD springs into action. HADD searches for any present people or animals that might have caused the event. It also tries to determine if the event might accomplish some goal. If agent candidates can be found, HADD registers the event as caused by agency and passes the word on to ToM, which then works out the motivations and thought processes that might have led the agent to bring about the event. If ToM can suggest the agent's desires and aims relevant to the event, it affirms to HADD that the event was goal directed, increasing HADD's confidence that agency has been discovered.

In the case of the silo explosion, we actually have a number of events that might get HADD jumping, but for the sake of clarity, I'll focus just on Doug getting out of the silo before the ultimate explosion. A physical object (Doug's body) moved up into the air and through a window over a dozen feet above the ground. Though an agent himself, Doug did not perceive his own agency to be responsible for this movement. Further, knowledge of human abilities would reject the possibility that he had leaped into the air under his own power. Because the movement of the physical object (Doug's body) cannot be readily explained in terms of simple mechanics or simple biological causation and because the movement was directed at a goal (the window), HADD searches for agency to account for the apparently goal-directed event. In this case, because "angel" was already a cultural concept that might (if believed) account for the detected agency, HADD's suggestion of agency was readily labeled "angel." Doug's negatively answered prayer and perhaps the suggestions of coworkers reinforced the identification of angels being responsible for the event, even though at the time of the event Doug did not consider himself a true believer in God or in angels.

Note that whether or not Doug believed in angels or that angels rescue people from silos is largely irrelevant to his attributing the event to the activity of angels. Suppose Doug had believed in God but not angels but had heard of angels taking care of people. Although he did not "believe in" angels prior to the event, HADD detected agency, and his memory for information about angels nonreflectively made them prime candidates of this agency. When reflectively forming a belief, angels made intuitive sense as the most likely explanation for the event. Thus, reflective belief in angels was strengthened.

For people disinclined to believe in angels or gods, it might be tempting to think that such an implicit thought process is odd or irrational. What is important to remember is that the system through which ideas become beliefs is not concerned with being "rational" or following some logic. It rapidly produces beliefs that produce intuitive satisfaction, resonating with the nonreflective beliefs that various mental tools produce.

Consider the angel attribution–versus–naturalistic counterexplanation. Perhaps an explosion lifted Doug up through the window and to the ground outside the silo before the final explosion and Doug's feeling of being lifted by the arms and hearing a voice were caused by a propane-induced hallucination and some memory distortion for the event. Though perhaps being a scientifically possible

explanation, it suffers numerous weaknesses from the perspective of intuitive reasoning. It requires believing the improbable (though not impossible) premise that
the voice and feeling of being grabbed by the arms was imagined or caused by the
same nonagent. It requires the improbable (though not impossible) supposition
that a propane explosion could blast a man up and out of a window without
harming him when such an explosion leveled a silo and barn. More critically, this
alternative requires an ability to tell HADD it was simply mistaken. HADD was
provided with all the relevant cues for attributing agency as the cause of the event,
and any other explanation must override the nonreflective belief that this was indeed the purposeful activity of an intentional being.

This system for forming beliefs likewise does not necessarily see the impossi-
bility of angels as a problem. At the moment HADD registers the nonreflective
belief that the event was caused by an agent, it does not specify what kind of agent
it is. Similarly, when mental tools find angels a reasonable candidate, they do not
notice that angels are counterintuitive. They notice only that what is known about
angels provides a good fit for the sort of agency HADD has detected. Even if the
counterintuitiveness of angels (for example, that they are invisible) factored in, being counterintuitive does not immediately cause disbelief. We know that lots of
counterintuitive things are real and do happen (such as the Venus's-flytrap, invisible germs killing people, human-engineered plants, and being able to speak with
someone on the other side of the world). Being counterintuitive may decrease the
likelihood of a reflective belief being formed, but if the counterintuitiveness increases the number of mental tools or the amount of nonreflective "evidence" for
the belief, the result is increasing the likelihood of reflective belief. The invisibility of angels satisfies the feeling of being grasped by the arms but seeing no one.
A visible agent would be even less credible in this situation.

HADD and Identifying Traces of Agency

Not all agents may be directly observed as objects or their actions observed as
events. Sometimes our best clues to agency having taken place are what agents leave
behind: their traces. Traces of people include roads, machines, books, signs,
houses, artwork, and footprints. Traces of animals include birds' nests, ground-
hogs' burrows, deer trails, and bears' scratches on trees. On seeing such traces,
HADD may recognize agency, though the process requires the help of other mental tools and is not as straightforward as in considering objects or events.

Our minds have numerous pattern detectors that organize visual information
into meaningful units. HADD remains on the lookout for patterns known to be
caused by agents. If this patterned information matches patterns (stored in memory, sort of a pattern file) known to be caused by agents, HADD detects agency

and alerts other mental tools, including ToM. Thus, dealing with *known* agent traces is the simplest and least interesting way in which HADD handles traces. Because we know the agents in question, they will not likely be attributed to superhuman agency and thus play little role in the acquisition or spread of god concepts. In fact, by early childhood we become so accustomed to dealing with human-made things—artifacts—that we develop mental tools that specially deal with artifacts without HADD's being included in the loop.[6]

More interesting is when a pattern is detected that appears to be purposeful or goal directed and, secondarily, does not appear to be caused by ordinary mechanical or biological causes. Such patterns may prompt HADD to attribute the traces to agency yet to be identified: unknown persons, animals, or space aliens, ghosts, or gods. Crop circles may serve as an appropriate illustration.

Over the past several decades in various locations around the world, people have reported geometric shapes and complex patterns appearing in grain fields, literally overnight. Such patterns have been called "crop circles." Frequently, the stalks of the plants have been bent over to yield the intricate designs visible from the air. People commonly attribute these patterns to the activity of superhuman agency—typically extraterrestrials but sometimes gods—and skeptics scramble for alternative explanations. But what makes these patterns seem to be the work of agents?

Crop circles contrast with their surroundings by approximating the sorts of purposeful patterns that people produce: smooth circular curves, straight lines, and clean angles, all surrounded by more naturally appearing plants. Such apparent order and purposefulness in the construction of the crop circle patterns excites HADD. Further, crop circles cannot be easily explained by natural mechanical or biological processes. That is, the creation of such patterns by gravity, wind, plant development, or other familiar processes appears unlikely on an intuitive level (as well as a reflective level). The inability to account for such apparently purposeful patterns through regular mechanistic or biological causation further motivates HADD to find agency behind the trace. Once HADD registers the crop circles as a trace of agency, it produces a nonreflective belief that the crop circles were left deliberately by someone.

When constructing a reflective belief, HADD's identification of the crop circles as intentionally caused by some kind of agent cannot be easily shaken. Indeed, few who see crop circles believe they were not caused by an agent. What is disputed is what kind of agent produced them: people or superhuman agency? Though the hypothesis that a person or persons produced the crop circles receives intuitive support from HADD and other mental tools, it does not fit perfectly. Intuitively, people create things for purposes. The purpose or functionality of the crop circles is unclear. Further, additional, expected traces of human activity, such as footprints or tire tracks, often aren't discovered. Finally, as solid, physical objects, humans may be observed acting, and the witnesses of crop circles do not report having seen anyone do the work. On an intuitive, nonreflective level, nonnatural, superhuman agents can avoid all these difficulties. Invisible agents could do the work unseen. More powerful agents could do the work from a remote location, leaving no auxiliary traces. Less familiar agents (such as extraterrestrials) might have purposes in creating the patterns that people would not readily appreciate. Given these observations, once some extraterrestrial agency or other superhuman agency is suggested, its (reflective) plausibility is reinforced by the nonreflective beliefs produced by the constellation of mental tools triggered by HADD.

Though the case of crop circles vividly illustrates what I call "traces," traces mentioned in religious discourse frequently have more subtle features. For instance, in the Judeo-Christian story of Gideon (Judges 6), Gideon asks God for proof that God will indeed use Gideon to deliver Israel. God motivates Gideon's trust by making a fleece dew covered while the surrounding ground is dry and then making the fleece dry while the ground is wet with dew. Though not resembling what we normally think of a symbolic communication, this too qualifies as a trace because Gideon saw the fleece's state as purposeful.

In identifying traces as the consequence of agency, HADD pays special attention to whether the trace (including objects) might be purposeful. This ability to discern purposefulness (accurately or inaccurately) sometimes carries the name *teleological reasoning* and permeates intuitive thought about artifacts and living things.[7] We do not know all the factors that contribute to something being perceived as purposeful by the mental tools that do this work. What cognitive scientists have shown us is that from the preschool years of childhood, we eagerly attend to how the shape or structure of things may be useful to people (allowing for our sophisticated development and use of tools) or useful for other things, such as plants and animals. Handles are good for gripping. Having thorns is good for repelling predators. As the possession of useful or purposeful features (such as in artifacts) typically signals design by some intentional agent (such as by humans), detection of purposefulness excites HADD. Purposefulness that cannot be attributed to natural agents (as is the case for people's houses and birds' nests) may be attributed to nonnatural agents. Thus, the presence of spines on a porcupine or the prehensile tail of a monkey could suggest a designer or a creator.[8]

I return to these issues briefly in chapter 5, but here I make one point of clarification. I do not mean to suggest that the notion of or belief in gods originates with noticing order or apparent purposefulness in the natural world. With the exception of very unusual cases such as crop circles, unlike HADD operating on events or objects, HADD's attribution of agency to traces probably serves to *rein-*

force rather than *stimulate* god concepts. People who have already heard about a god might see a HADD trace as supportive of that concept and thereby encourage belief. But with few exceptions, seeing a HADD trace is unlikely to prompt the wholesale invention of a god. After all, even the Psalmist writes, "The heavens are telling of the glory of God; And their expanse is declaring the work of his hands," but not that it is by the heavens that God is made known.

HADD's Flexibility with Context

The degree of HADD's sensitivity varies, depending on personal and immediate contexts. By personal contexts, I refer to individual histories and dispositions. People who are especially afraid of particular agents, perhaps because of previous experiences, might be more apt to detect an agent whether or not they are there. Someone with acute fear of spiders who feels a gentle tickle on her neck would be more likely to assume immediately and react as if a spider were there than someone without such a phobia. Similarly, someone who once was bitten by a venomous snake in tall grass might be primed to react to a garden hose as if it were a snake. People who believe in ghosts are more likely to see ghosts than nonbelievers. Being a believer—or even merely open to believing—in a god makes one more sensitive to detecting the god's action or presence. For instance, a nonbeliever might find no reason to see divine intervention as a reasonable explanation for surviving the silo explosion.

In addition to what I have called the personal context, the immediate context also helps determine HADD's sensitivity and likelihood to detect agency. I refer primarily to the *urgency* of the situation for survival or at least for the success or failure of activities that might suggest survival to our prehistorically created minds. Situations in which we are desperately searching for possible prey or in which we suspect we might be prey for someone or something else or we are desperately in need of finding other people ratchet up the importance of HADD detecting agency given very little information. Missing agency in such urgent situations could prove disastrous, much more disastrous than when we are secure and well fed. To illustrate, imagine that a person walking through the woods hears what might be a rustling of leaves and cracking of twigs nearby. For the person on an afternoon stroll in a perfectly safe park with no large animals, such an occasion might be easily dismissed as "just the wind" or ignored completely. For a person having the same visual and auditory experience but out sport hunting for deer, the noise is likely to suggest the presence of a deer—HADD activated. For a person subsistence hunting for deer, HADD would be even more likely to shout, "There's a deer!"—metaphorically, of course. People not hunting who were just sauntering through the woods but minutes before had heard that a serial killer was loose in these woods would have their HADDs screaming at them.

Given that HADD becomes more sensitive in situations of urgency, it is no surprise that the most salient examples of misattributing agency are "bump in the night" scenarios. Likewise, people who live in situations in which their survival is more precarious often have both personal and immediate contexts encouraging the easy and rapid detection of agents. People in these contexts, who cannot easily attribute this agency to known humans, may be especially prone to detect ghosts, spirits, and gods in their midst. Not surprisingly, then, in more traditional societies, such as those tied to subsistence hunting or farming, where life is filled with nonhuman dangers, life is also filled with forest spirits, ghosts, witches, and ancestor spirits constantly and obviously at work.

Finding Supernatural Agents and Reinforcing Beliefs

Given HADD's eagerness to identify things as agents and to find agency around us, it is no wonder that we yell at our cars and computers, assume that the creaking of a settling house is caused by intruders, and easily understand colors and lines on film as actual characters with a rich mental life—a life for which we have no direct evidence. As suggested previously, such eagerness also contributes to generating and believing in supernatural agents such as gods.

Actual experiences—seeing a shadowy figure purposefully moving and then suddenly disappearing, being saved from an exploding building, or finding signs or messages not created by any human or animal—may spark people to suggest and subsequently believe in gods, spirits, and other superhuman beings. The nonreflective beliefs generated by HADD, ToM, and other mental tools working together to make sense of unusual objects, events, or traces may become reflective beliefs when satisfactory alternative explanations fail to arise. Perhaps someone walking through the ruins of the old dairy saw something that looked like a humanoid figure and heard the sound of an unseen goat in the figure's general direction just before some debris fell dangerously close. Thanks to HADD, that person then acquired a sketchy and perhaps tentative belief in the Chivo Man.

But this function of HADD does not explain religious beliefs all by itself. Such events may be few and far between, arising mostly in high-urgency situations. Once things have calmed down, many of HADD's detections of agency turn out to be unfounded. They amount to false positives. "I thought I heard an intruder in the house, but it was just the wind." "I thought I saw a ghostly figure, but it was just a sheet on the clothesline." After all, HADD's initial detection of agency and the subsequent agent-based reasoning of ToM and other mental tools sometimes become disengaged, as when I discover it is not an insect crawling on my leg but a blade of grass brushing against it. If HADD couldn't be successfully disengaged, its hypersensitivity would lead to survival difficulties and not advantages. If the tiger I thought I saw in the brush turns out to be a rock, I'd better be able to respond to the rock as a rock and not continue to fear it might pounce on me. Otherwise, I will expend lots of energy unnecessarily.

Even if HADD confidently and unrepentantly detected superhuman agents on a fairly common basis, these beliefs would not give rise to religion or any shared concepts that might be called cultural without these beliefs being able to successfully spread to other people. The *transmission* dynamics governing MCI ideas may help, but HADD does encourage the spread of these beliefs as well as their generation.

Even a temporary activation of HADD may promote memory for and belief in an agent. Consider the following situation. Jeff is hunting for deer in a forest. At one point he hears some noise in a thicket some fifty meters away. His HADD, being more sensitive than usual because of the predatory context, suggests a deer in the brush. Jeff stops, carefully evaluates the surroundings, looks around and listens for additional evidence of a deer, and finds none. He shrugs off the idea that a deer was in the brush (maybe it was the wind? maybe it was a squirrel?) and continues on his way. Some exhausting hours later, no longer excited and not even interested in finding a deer, Jeff passes through the same thicket in which he had once suspected an agent. Because the identification of agency was never resolved, he looks around for additional evidence for what caused the rustling. He finds deer hair and droppings. Reflectively, Jeff believes a deer had indeed been there, and part of the reason (though not even most of the reason) was that HADD had told him so hours before. Perhaps HADD had been right after all.

Indeed, HADD may be most likely to find agency if given ambiguous inputs in urgent or frightening contexts, and HADD's agent detection may be subsequently disengaged or left without identifying a satisfactory agent (Hmmm, I thought someone was there . . .). As Jeff's deer hunt illustrates, the nonreflective belief HADD produces in the heat of the moment may leave a memory for agency that is still drawn on to form reflective beliefs at later times. Even this unlabeled or nonbelieved HADD-produced experience may reinforce subsequent belief.

HADD-produced experiences may contribute to the transmission of an idea and a belief in it before or after exposure to the idea. While passing through the haunted dairy, Lupe's HADD "notices" an unseen agent there, but Lupe reflectively dismisses it. If at a later time she hears about the Chivo Man living at the haunted dairy, she may recollect her HADD experience, increasing the likelihood of remembering and believing the Chivo Man tale. In this way, Lupe's HADD experience, plus later exposure to the superhuman concept, leads to belief. But recall that in the example of Steve coming to believe in the Chivo Man (chapter 2), the process worked in just the opposite way. Steve had heard but not believed in Chivo Man until he had a HADD experience consistent with the Chivo Man tale. Both before and after exposure to a superhuman agent concept, HADD may encourage belief even when the HADD experience itself was not sufficient to produce an enduring belief on its own.

At this point, if you have been raised in Europe or North America, you might be thinking that some half-person chimera such as the Chivo Man has little to do with belief in gods. Not so. Comparative religionists and anthropologists tell us that when looking at religions around the world, the category "gods" includes many chimeras and other beings that derive from nonhuman things. Mountains, trees, rocks, statues, and countless other things, often not at all resembling humans, play critical roles in religious systems and are worshiped, petitioned, and feared.[9] In the Chivo Man example, behaviors beginning to suggest religion may begin to arise once Steve and Lupe start sharing and comparing their accounts with others. It may begin with simply avoiding unnecessarily entering the haunted dairy—regarding it as something like sacred ground. (Indeed, this may in fact be the case in the small Californian community near where the Chivo Man is said to dwell.) I could develop a similar example using an ephemeral humanlike being to whom people offer gifts to avoid wrath and incur blessings. Some HADD experience encourages the concept's generation; others who have heard (but not necessarily believed) in the spirit subsequently have HADD experiences that encourage belief and spread of the idea. Over time, a critical mass of such transmissions and HADD experiences cement belief in the spirit as part of local consciousness and a set of behaviors acknowledging the belief develop. The spirit is now a god.

But it is true that a superhuman being—though perhaps a god in some minimal sense—does not always become part of the social life that might be properly labeled "religion." In later chapters, I present some additional factors that help take Chivo Man from a minor cultural belief to the status of a god.

HADD, ToM, and Age and Sex Differences in Religiosity

Earlier in this chapter, I explained that if ToM can suggest the agent's desires and aims relevant to the event, it affirms to HADD that the event was goal directed, increasing HADD's confidence that agency has been discovered. Thus, HADD's work is not in isolation, and ToM's flexibility and readiness to explain subtle signs of agency encourage HADD's touchiness. A relatively unimaginative ToM might refuse a "detection" of agency from HADD, in essence replying to HADD, "I can't make heads or tails of why an agent would do that. Are you sure you really detected agency?"

One remarkably stable finding across religious traditions is that women tend to be more religiously involved and committed than men.[10] For instance, they tend to pray more than men, attend worship services more regularly than men, and voluntarily read scripture more than men. Undoubtedly, many factors contribute to this sex difference, and one of these factors may be the relationship between ToM and HADD. Psychologists have noted that, in general, women may have more active ToM's than men. They more readily reason about the beliefs, desires, motivations, emotions, perspectives, and intentions of others and use this ToM reasoning to make decisions and negotiate social exchanges. In fact, autism, a disorder characterized in part by a severe inability to understand others' minds, has been called an extreme form of "male brainedness" and occurs much more frequently in males than females.[11] If this suspected gender difference in ToM activity is so, we would expect women to be more religious than men. While both men and women might have a similar rate of HADD detecting agency around that might get attributed to gods, men's ToM's might be stingier about affirming such a detection of supernatural agency. Women might be more able to readily explain and incorporate HADD's detections of agency in terms of superhuman activity than men.

A similar account could be offered for the finding that people's religiosity tends to increase with age.[12] Again, numerous factors (such as an increasing awareness of one's own mortality) may contribute to this effect. Here is another possible factor. Some experimental evidence suggests that part of the wisdom of the elderly is an increase (relative to young adults, for instance) of social intelligence.[13] While researchers have found that aging slows some thought processes and reduces certain types of memory, it also appears to increase our ability to reason about the mental states of others and thus to effectively address social dilemmas. In other words, in contrast to some other reasoning faculties, ToM might continue to get stronger, more flexible, more creative, and more ambitious with age. Consequently, increases in religiosity with age might be (at least in part) attributable to ToM's increased willingness to entertain HADD's detections of agency and labeling them as the result of divine activity.

The Spreading Belief in Gods

For an idea or concept to be considered "religious," it must be shared among a group of individuals. One person believing in a superhuman being doesn't do the job. If no one else believes, the idea is just odd, not religious. Consequently, a critical part of accounting for god concepts and other religious ideas is explaining how they successfully spread from individual mind to individual mind and become believed by those individuals. Thus far, I have offered two ways in which ordinary mental tools encourage the belief in and spread of religious concepts.

First, concepts that may be regarded as MCI strike a balance between meeting the assumptions of categorizers and describers and possessing enough violations that make them interesting and having rich inferential potential. This balance motivates us to attend to them, remember them, and talk about them and makes them easy to reproduce accurately. That they satisfy the bulk of intuitive assumptions of categorizers and describers likewise makes them largely credible.

Second, our mental tools pay special attention to agency in the world around us. We find explanations that end with appeal to an agent's desire very attractive and powerful. Consequently, MCI agent concepts often enjoy a great ability to explain, predict, and make sense of memories, experiences, and other ideas. That is, MCI agent concepts (as compared with other agent concepts) are more likely to excite a large number of mental tools, further enhancing these agents' credibility. One particular mental tool, HADD, is quick to find agency in the environment. This survival-enhancing disposition encourages the production of superhuman agent concepts in many situations and makes MCI agent concepts even more salient, believable, and likely to be spread by anchoring them to personal experiences.

In the next chapter, I explore in more detail some of the additional mental tools or systems of tools that god concepts (and other superhuman agent concepts) activate, thereby enhancing gods' credibility.

Notes

1. Guthrie (1993).
2. Guthrie does not use the term ADD or HADD. These are acronyms that I introduce to capture and develop Guthrie's observations (Barrett, 2000).
3. For a review of this work in adults, see Scholl and Tremoulet (2000); see also Bassili (1976); Berry, Misovich, Keen, and Baron (1992); White (1995); and White and Milne (1999). For examples of developmental studies, see Gelman, Durgin, and Kaufman (1995); Gergely and Csibra (2003); Gergely, Nadasdy, Csibra, and Biro (1995); Leslie (1995); Premack (1990); Premack and Premack (1995); and Rochat, Morgan, and Carpenter (1997).
4. Classic studies demonstrating the seductiveness of simple movements in geometric shapes to trigger overzealous agent attributions (see Heider & Simmel, 1944; Michotte, 1963). Both found that adults readily attribute beliefs, desires, emotions, and even genders and personality traits to dots under certain conditions.
5. Barrett and Johnson (2003).
6. For more on mental systems concerned with artifacts, see Bloom (1998).
7. In addition to Bloom (1998), see Keil (1989, 1992, 1995) and Kelemen (1999a, 1999b, 1999c, 1999d).
8. Kelemen (in press).
9. For examples, see Lawson (1985).
10. Paloutzian (1996).
11. Baron-Cohen (2002); Happe (1995).
12. Paloutzian (1996).
13. Happe, Winner, and Brownell (1998).

BEING MINIMALLY COUNTERINTUITIVE, god concepts demand attention but are easy to remember and communicate to others faithfully. In addition, our tendency to rapidly detect agency in our environments and further to credit these agents with a host of mental states helps generate and encourage the spread of god concepts. Being agents, gods possess great inferential potential—the ability to explain or account for various events and phenomena. In this chapter, I turn to a number of domains in which agents—particularly the right kind of superhuman agents—mesh well with ordinary reasoning, making god concepts even more attractive.

In chapters 2 and 3, I described how god concepts amount to minimally counterintuitive (MCI) agent concepts. More specifically, god concepts come in three basic varieties (or some combination thereof). First, gods may be agents with unusual counterintuitive biological properties. The ancient Greeks understood their gods as having fairly ordinary physical properties and minds. They even ate food. But their bodies were immortal—a counterintuitive biological property. Second, gods may be agents with counterintuitive physical properties. For instance, people conceive of ghosts as having fairly ordinary minds but of being distinctive because they have no material bodies. Note that once a body is eliminated from the picture, biological assumptions evaporate as well; but because biological assumptions apply only to bodies, immortality in a ghost cannot properly be considered an additional counterintuitive feature. Third, gods may be physical objects—such as statues or volcanoes—that have agency added to them, including minds very similar to human minds. In African tribal religions, natural objects, such as trees, often possess minds and the ability to bless or curse people.[1]

Chapters 2 and 3 described how mental tools encourage nonreflective (and subsequently reflective) belief in gods of all three classes. In this chapter, I offer a sampling of ways in which ordinary mental activities further encourage belief in gods, primarily gods in the second class, that is, those that have counterintuitive physical properties. Usually this means gods that have no material bodies or are invisible. These agents with counterintuitive physical properties may be easily integrated into thought in three particular areas that are commonly associated with religions around the world: 1) social interactions, including those with moral overtones; 2) incidences of fortune or misfortune; and 3) human death.

Gods' invisibility or immateriality promotes gods' connection to areas of social interactions, especially those concerned with moral judgment. In turn, thinking about social interactions in terms of godly perspectives reinforces belief in the gods. A host of mental tools find (nonreflective) belief in gods satisfying and generate social judgments on this basis, providing any subsequent reflective belief making with ample fodder for the gods' credibility.

Gods' unusual physical properties also facilitate their connection to incidences of peculiar fortune or misfortune. Unlike human agents, who typically must be visibly present to cause help or harm, gods may act in a more covert manner, making them candidates to answer why some things happen to certain people.

As I argue in this chapter, the death of humans—especially loved ones—may present conflicting outputs from largely unconsciously operating mental tools. These mixed messages may give rise to or at least encourage beliefs in life after death and concepts of ghosts and spirit ancestors, two of the more commonly believed-in types of gods.

Gods and Social Interactions

As social beings, people have numerous mental tools that facilitate smooth social interaction. The hypersensitive agency detection device (HADD) and the Theory of Mind (ToM) are two such mental tools, but they only start the identification and elaboration of potential social partners. Anthropologists and psychologists have also suggested that we have mental tools responsible for such activities as moral reasoning,[2] identifying who has high social status so that we might learn from them to improve our own standing,[3] and reasoning about others as members of groups or classes and not just as individuals.[4] We may also have a mental tool or tools responsible for social exchanges and activities conditional on social qualifications.[5] As with the mental tools described in previous chapters, these mental tools operate largely without conscious awareness but do a tremendous amount of complex reasoning automatically so that our conscious mental faculties need not be cluttered with such matters.

These social mental tools have no difficulty reasoning about gods, even when the gods are never seen. Potential social agents typically first receive identification from HADD and description by ToM. As these two mental tools operate smoothly with gods as agents in question, so do the other social mental tools. Not even gods' invisibility or absence causes any problems. An important ability for smooth social interaction is the ability to imagine and consider past and future and real and possible social interactions. We need to be able to reason that "if so and so does such and such, then I'll do this and that; but if so and so were to do. . . ." Such reasoning requires that we can think about the mental states and actions of agents that are not even present, maybe even agents we have never seen. Such a capability also makes reasoning about gods, even unseen ones, quite natural.

Gods and Morality

One typical marker of true gods—superhuman agents that centrally matter to religious systems—is their inclusion in matters of moral judgment. Contrary to what many believe, religions do not invent morality wholesale and insert gods as the final arbiters over right and wrong. Rather, people the world over seem to have massively overlapping senses of what constitutes moral behavior. This regularity across cultures casts grave doubt on the alleged arbitrariness or relativity of morality.

For instance, taboos against incest may be found in essentially any society. Likewise, prohibitions against adultery, stealing, and murder assume similar forms everywhere. I do not mean to say that these prohibitions have no differences or do not take slightly different forms from place to place. In some places, what some of us might call murder is deemed acceptable as part of "warfare." In some communities, stealing may be congratulated when perpetrated against enemies but severely punished if performed against one's own people. However, the fact is that these moral codes governing sexual and social relations, aggressive behavior, and deception are not simply invented out of thin air like a rule against playing with spherical objects or a taboo against standing on one foot might be. Out of the innumerable possible types of moral rules that might be created, only a small number become widespread within and across cultures and carry normative gravity.[6]

Sociobiologists and other evolutionary human scientists have argued that part of our biologically endowed mental equipment is a system of mental tools that generate skeletal moral intuitions. Let's call this *intuitive morality* because these moral intuitions operate largely below conscious awareness but consciously give us an intuitive sense that something is right or wrong. Intuitive morality provides the prerequisite "instincts" for living in communities harmoniously and providing for some uniformity in behavioral expectations. It has been argued that groups of individuals with these moral inclinations enjoyed survival advantages over those who live (what we would call) immorally: always acting selfishly, fighting, stealing, cheating, murdering. Consequently, the vast majority of people today have the same sorts of moral sensibilities.[7]

Scholars sometimes criticize such evolutionary accounts on a number of fronts. Some question the viability of group-selection evolutionary accounts. Some doubt whether moral behavior really provides selective advantages. Others point to the dissociation between moral intuitions and moral behavior. After all, people do not always behave morally and recognize the fact. Still other scholars want to know better how negotiations take place between competing moral impulses, as when a drive for self-preservation competes with an impulse of noble self-sacrifice or when an aversion to deception confronts an aversion to hurting another's feelings. What mechanism judges between the impulses, and where does it come from? Despite reservations with a particular account for recurrent moral sensibilities across cultures, what seems indisputable (at least to me) is that such systematic sensibilities exist.

Indeed, when individuals dispute an application of these basic moral rules, the challenge usually takes the form of qualifying but *not* negating the rules. For example, someone might say, "It was okay to lie to my mother about where I was going [breaking a moral prohibition about deception] because it concealed plans for her surprise birthday party [a greater good showing love and affection]." What people do not say is that "lying is fine; calling it 'immoral' is just plain silly." People also do not suggest that moral rules could be changed: "Let's make murder okay." Such a strong, willing adherence to the normative force of these moral rules, even without any consciously held reasons for them, suggests that their origins are deeper than mere invention.[8]

Another aspect of moral thought that hints at the naturalness of morality lies in the way people have moral disagreements. If two or more people disagree about proper moral behavior in some situation, they typically do not argue about the moral principles themselves, that is, whether they should be followed, but disagreements typically revolve around the facts of the case. "If you could see *my* side of things, you would understand." Systems of civil law in democratic nations reflect the importance of getting the facts straight and hearing from both sides. The perceived importance of the facts in a dispute reveals again that people are generally *moral realists*. That is, we understand moral laws to be immutable and nonarbitrary. We believe that if everyone had full access to the relevant facts of a social interaction (including actions taken, motivations, and intentions), then they would agree on what constitutes moral or immoral behavior.[9]

That facts matter provides a natural connection to gods, as Boyer has suggested.[10] By virtue of their invisibility (or other counterintuitive physical properties), gods may be anywhere at any given moment. Consequently, even if they have not been specifically attributed super-vision, superhearing, or superknowledge, they may be witnesses to any human actions. Assuming that gods do know what you or anyone else has done is much easier than trying to determine just what this invisible agent might and might not know. Hence, we often credit gods with superknowledge.

At this point, I should note that people in some cultures do not regard their gods as particularly smart or superknowledgeable. Not all gods can read minds, and few know absolutely everything. For instance, anthropologist Harvey Whitehouse reports that the Baining people on East New Britain Island of Papua New Guinea have two classes of deities. The ancestor spirits read minds and generally know about the people's affairs, but the *sega*, or forest spirits, have no such special powers beyond regular observation of people acting in the forest.[11] Likewise, anthropologist and psychologist Nicola Knight has noted that among the Yucatek Maya of southern Mexico, various deities enjoy differential access to people's activities from the all-knowing Catholic God, to the *Chiichi*, who do not know much more than a peeping Tom would.[12] Nevertheless, generally, those gods that matter most to religious systems do know a lot more than the average person about a special group of information: strategic information. Indeed, in both the Pomio Kivung example and the Maya example, it is the more informed gods that matter most to the religious systems. Boyer calls strategic information any information that people might draw on to plan or modify their social interactions. Typically, this information relates, in one way or another, to survival and reproductive resources. Thus, gods more frequently know about who is stealing from whom and who is having sexual relations with whom instead of just how many ants are on a particular leaf on a particular tree in a particular South American country. Even gods that we believe on a reflective, theological level know absolutely everything, including the count of ants in some place, do not know absolutely everything on a nonreflective level. We simply cannot understand, in any useful sense, what that means. What we can nonreflectively believe is that a theologically omniscient god knows everything we care about, including everything relevant to morality applied to ourselves and others.

How Strategic Information Encourages the Spread of God Concepts

Understanding gods as knowing about what we care about comes easily, simply by the way our minds work and by the small number of counterintuitive properties gods possess. That gods know so much makes accounts of them even more likely to be remembered, pondered, and communicated to others. Why so? First, because if they do know so much about us and others, they hold the potential to be both powerful allies and dangerous enemies. As social beings that thrive on information, we gravitate toward sources of strategic information that we might be able to access. We also may carry some anxiety about individuals who have personal information about us that might be shared with others. Boyer compares this relationship with gods to our relationship with gossip. People (whether or not they believe they should be) are drawn to gossip for the information it may provide but fear gossip for the information it may reveal about ourselves.

A second reason that superknowing gods demand more attention than some other counterintuitive beings is because of their status. Some cognitive anthropologists have argued that social beings have a critical ability to rapidly determine who it is we should learn from and imitate in a community,[13] the best being those who have high social status and thus high amounts of material resources that support survival and reproduction. Consequently, once the mental tool responsible for determining social status—the social status monitor—detects high-status individuals, we find ourselves paying great attention to them and trying to stay on their good sides. Gods, having access to critical social information, may be worthy beings to learn from or worthy of fear. Thus, the gods, if they exist, may be worth great attention and demonstrations of positive regard.

Finally, as suggested previously, because gods have strategic information, they may be guarantors of moral behavior. If someone does something wrong, even in secret, a god would know and could punish the wrongdoer. If someone does something exceptionally good, a god would know about it and could reward the behavior. By having full access to a dispute with moral considerations, a god would know who is in the right and could mete out justice or sympathize with those who have been wronged. When no one else sides with me, at least God does.[14]

That the mere idea of a god may weave itself intricately into social events and personal concerns makes god concepts inferentially rich and capable of activating large numbers of mental tools that may nonreflectively believe in the gods if they become accustomed to reasoning about them. A critical point here is that because humans have the ability to imagine possible states of affairs and possible agents, one need not believe that a god does exist for the notion of a god to inhabit mental space. Just being thought about and their potential connection to social activities makes them more likely to be considered and talked about and thereby spread than other counterintuitive concepts. However, if someone is inclined to believe in a given god (perhaps because of some of the factors mentioned in chapters 2 and 3), that the god may activate mental tools dealing with social interactions and morality would only enhance nonreflective belief. Remember the principle that the more mental tools with which an idea fits, the more likely it is to become a belief. A god that knows about human affairs (as opposed to one that knows only the number of ants on a leaf, for example) fits with a vast array of mental tools.

Because of endowed superknowledge or their invisibility, gods have knowledge of human activities relevant to human social interaction. That they have such knowledge makes them attractive to think about and places them as potential moral arbitrators. Both these factors would encourage the notion of these gods to spread, to be communicated with others, and to occupy our imaginations. The more they occupy our thought and the more interesting the roles we can imagine them playing in social life, the more plausible they seem. Each time we import a god into our moral reasoning or reasoning about human interactions ("What would God think about what he did?"), our mental tools gain fluency in reasoning with the assumption that the god exists. Nonreflective belief strengthens. But why would anyone connect gods with morality in the first place? In the next section, I turn to this question.

Fortune, Misfortune, and Gods

As we go through life, many wonderful and horrible things happen to us and those around us. Friends die young and tragically, whereas others avoid seemingly certain death. We get job promotions we didn't expect; we get fired when we least expect it. We lose money; we win a lottery. Some days, all the lights turn green for us, but on others they all turn red. When such events happen to strangers, they are easily chalked up to "dumb luck" or "chance." But when they happen to us or those we love, such cold, statistical reasoning seems unsatisfying. We seem compelled to ask, what does it all mean? for what reason? why did it happen?

Such questions are not simply because people are poor at causal or probabilistic reasoning. Actually, people tabulate the concurrence of events and detect the relationship between factors fairly well. For instance, we can tell which skies may bring rain and which will not. We determine who the best cooks are after just a few holiday family gatherings. With limited exposure, we learn what sort of body language of dogs suggests amiable versus aggressive encounters.

Because people are so good at tabulating regularities, however, we often overestimate the connection between factors. We find correlations that simply aren't there and find exceptions to a pattern more exceptional than they perhaps should appear.[15] A survivor of an illness remarks that the type of illness he had has a 90 percent chance of death, so his survival was a miracle. Of course, 90 percent chance of death leaves ten out of one hundred people surviving. Would we want to say that all ten survivals are miracles? Probably not. But to the person who survived such harrowing odds and to their family and friends, such an event may *seem* very much a miracle. And there is nothing (necessarily) sloppy about such thinking. If something happens that is improbable, appealing to some statistical argument or "chance" as a reason for the event is really no reason at all. If the odds of winning a lottery are ten million to one and I win, explaining that someone had to win is no reason *I* won; it does not explain why I won. What statisticians and science-minded people should assert is that there is nothing to be explained. An unlikely event happening is just an unlikely event happening.[16] Of course, such an objection rings hollow to the person who has just enjoyed a stroke of "luck" or suffered an unlikely tragedy. As with everything else in life, we automatically, often nonconsciously, look for an explanation of why things happen to us (or people close to us), and "stuff just happens" is no explanation. Gods, by virtue of their strange physical properties and their mysterious superpowers, make fine candidates for causes of many of these unusual events.[17]

Of course, not all events may be explained in terms of gods' activity. Events that have immediately identifiable physical, biological, human, or other known causes won't typically be attributed to gods. That an unsupported object falls to the ground, that a teased dog bites, and that ample water and sunlight help crops grow well require no appeal to the supernatural.

Likewise, many misfortunes (or fortunes) in the modern world may be easily seen as the fault of people or human institutions. As described in chapter 3, when regular mechanical or biological causation fails to produce a palatable explanation for an event or state of affairs, HADD suspects that some kind of agency is at play. When appeals to human agency seem to do the job and are salient, then that is where credit lies. The person got well because of a "miracle drug," not because of a miraculous divine intervention. The doctor had particular skill. "It's the government's fault."

But if human agency is not such a good fit, as when an event requires power beyond known human agency, then the gods may be an intuitive explanation. We know that people cannot cause lightning to strike particular individuals. When the doctors say there is no hope of recovery from advanced and widespread cancer but the cancer vanishes overnight, we know human agency is not the cause. Even when something fairly mundane, such as the opening of a door, happens in a way that mechanics does not seem a reasonable explanation and no visible or auditory evidence of human presence is available, a god may seem a reasonable cause.

Often unconsciously, we try to make sense of our surroundings: what causes what, what something might indicate or mean. When our mental tools responsible for mechanistic or biological reasoning fail, HADD looks for agency. If human agency renders a satisfactory explanation, our search for causes stops. If human agency is not a good fit, a god may be an intuitively satisfying fit. These unconscious processes become the basis for reflective beliefs. In this way, gods, by virtue of being agents with special properties, become invoked as causes.

However, gods acting willy-nilly every time something otherwise inexplicable happens would not be satisfying. Gods don't just act whenever we can't explain it. Why in the world would they? Appeals to human agency as causes are satisfying because we can understand their actions as motivated or *caused* by intentions. Beliefs and desires of others make for good explanations because no further reasons for action are needed. Why, then, would gods heal people, strike them with lightning, or help them win the lottery? To answer this question, we return to our discussion about morality.

Connecting Fortune, Misfortune, and Morality

Many behavioral scientists have described the hypersociality of people. It isn't just that we are capable of, desire, or have a propensity toward social interaction. We are fundamentally social beings, designed for sociality.[18] Much as how we have a mental tool that hypersensitively detects agency (HADD) to explain the environment, we likewise seem to be prone to detect social causes for fortune or misfortune whenever possible.

Social causes amount to guiding principles for intentional agents' interaction. Thus, if Louis gives Clause money for some food, we fully expect Clause to give Louis something in return. No direct appeal to the beliefs and desires of Clause are necessary to predict or explain his behavior. Our social exchange regulator (another largely unconsciously operating mental tool) rapidly learns give-and-take regularities and then generates inferences on the basis of these principles. The social exchange regulator also tracks qualifications or contingencies on certain exchanges. For instance, in the United States, the ability to vote for public officials depends on at least two conditions: being at least eighteen years old and being a registered voter, with age being a prerequisite for registration. The social exchange regulator easily registers these qualifications and enables us to understand the nature of them quite easily. If someone showed up at a voting station and the official turned her away saying, "You're not registered," we easily understand why the transaction did not take place.[19]

The social exchange regulator cooperates with our intuitive morality to justify certain rewards and punishments. When Bruce morally wrongs Mingfa, we fully understand Mingfa acting in a retaliatory manner. Social exchange almost demands it. But when Margaret does something nice for Jennifer and Jennifer exchanges cruelty for the kindness, we immediately detect something deeply wrong with Jennifer's behavior and probably found it quite unexpected. Intuitively, we understand that good behavior should be rewarded and that immoral behavior earns punishments. Such morality-based exchange typically happens in the interactions of peers and parents with children. It should come as no surprise that we may readily apply such reasoning to gods.[20]

We anticipate parents to reward children for good behavior and punish them for bad behavior, but what happens when parents do not know about the children's behavior? We expect kindness to be repaid with kindness and treachery to conjure punishment when peers interact, but what happens if the kindness is secretive or the treachery goes unnoticed by other people? This is where the gods may step in.

As discussed previously, gods, by virtue of special powers (such as reading minds or simply knowing "everything") or special physical properties (such as being invisible), may know what people do even in secret. If I steal something from a neighbor but am never caught by a human, a god may still know about the transgression and punish it. If I secretively give gifts to my neighbor but am never caught by a human, a god may still know about the act of kindness and reward it. Easily understanding this *potential* role of the gods in human moral behaviors promotes the connection between fortune, misfortune, and the activity of the gods.

Similarly, as agents who may interact with people, gods may engage in their own social exchanges. If gods have strategic information that is valuable to me, I might try to get the gods to share this information with me. Or perhaps I would like the gods to protect me from harm. Or I would like them to prosper my crops. To get something of value from someone else, I usually have to pay some kind of price (exchange), or I have to have an established relationship that allows for free giving and receiving as in a close friendship or familial relationship. Such (automatic and largely nonconscious) reasoning might prompt me to make offerings to the gods or to alter my behavior in ways that please them. Conversely, I may offend the gods by wronging them directly.[21] Perhaps I have spoken badly about them or stolen someone else's gift to them or broken some other rule of engagement.

When something strikingly unfortunate happens to us, we and those close to us are prone to ask why. Out of the blue, it would be unusual for anyone to reason, "When do bad things happen to people? When they have done something to deserve it. Who could grant such an unusual punishment? Someone with superpowers and someone who knows about the evil that has been done. Who has such abilities? God." Even the nonconscious function of mental tools wouldn't provide such reasoning without prompts. But our mental tools very well may 1) look for a cause for surprising misfortune, 2) incline toward agentive/social explanations related to reward/punishment exchanges, but 3) require that a candidate agent could reasonably know about the evil that was done, even in secret, and has the power to punish. With these biases in place, the suggestion that a god could be responsible for the ill that has befallen someone possesses great intuitive plausibility, is likely to be remembered and transmitted, and thus is a strong candidate for a recurring explanation for misfortune.

Take the following example from a hypothetical agricultural village. A family experiences a series of devastating events: chickens die, wild boars destroy crops, and children fall ill. Though such misfortunes happen all the time, for all of them to befall one family within a period of a couple of days leads the family and neighbors to wonder what wrong they have committed for which the ancestor spirits might be punishing them. Given the supposed properties of the ancestor spirits and the intuitive impetus to find a reason for the events, some connection to the spirits makes a lot of sense.[22]

The same argument applies to unusual fortune. Let's return to the story from chapter 3 of Doug, who miraculously survived the silo explosion. Because three elements of this event (being unharmed by a violent explosion, being safely lifted out of a second-story window and to the ground below just before a more devastating explosion, and being unharmed by normally fatal levels of toxic gases) may not be readily explained in terms of normal causal processes familiar to our mental tools, Doug and his coworkers' minds scrambled to find an explanation. Given the biases of our mental tools to look for agentive/social explanations and the knowledge of God (and/or angels) as a qualified candidate, the suggestion that God was responsible for saving Doug seemed plausible to everyone close to the incident. But I understate: God seemed like the *only* plausible explanation.

Consider one more example. Anthropologist Scott Atran has recounted the following sort of incident in Central America among the Maya people. Bitten by an extremely dangerous venomous snake, a Maya hunter consulted the forest spirits for help. He refused medical aid from the anthropologist and instead "listened" for the forest spirits to tell him which plants to use as a remedy. After consulting the forest spirits, he gathered a few choice plants, applied them, and fully recovered from the bite. In a reportedly common case such as this, a direct appeal to gods is followed directly by great fortune. Concluding that the forest spirits saved the man's life makes great intuitive sense. Given the way our minds operate, to think anything else would be peculiar and aberrant and require explanation.

The properties gods typically have encourage us to incorporate gods into thinking about fortune and misfortune. They provide much-desired explanations for why peculiar and otherwise inexplicable things happen. But this tendency to incorporate gods into thinking about fortune and misfortune in turn reinforces belief in gods. Each time we satisfactorily understand an episode as being the work of a god, another memory is created affirming the existence of the god, and the mental tools responsible for such problem solving have more tightly woven the existence of the god into its operating assumptions. Nonreflective belief gets affirmed. Reflective belief gains reinforcement.

Life after Death

Death may be considered a special class of misfortune. The same analysis as used for other forms of misfortune applies to the death of a loved one or one's own imminent death, perhaps with additional salience. Other misfortunes may sometimes carry some ambiguity regarding their gravity and whether they *really* count as misfortune. Death does not. Like all animals, humans have an instinctual, bodily as well as mental, aversion to death. And perhaps greater than for all other animals, death of other people close to us creates powerful emotional experiences: emptiness, loneliness, anger, regret, and fear. Thus, more than perhaps any other type of misfortune, death cries out for an explanation, and the work of the gods lies in wait as the answer.

Additionally, death may encourage religious thought regarding ghosts and ancestor spirits even more directly. You see, the way that our minds handle the death of others, especially those we know well, makes belief in life after death (in some form or another) nearly inevitable on a cultural level.[23]

Psychologists and anthropologists have begun careful examination of how, from a very young age, our minds make sense of death. Though this work remains fairly new and requires additional development, initial findings provocatively point to life-after-death notions arising naturally from two ways minds work. The first path to belief in ghosts or spirits concerns the two separate mental tools that must deal with death of a person. The second way involves our ability to imagine what it might be like to be dead.

Biological versus Psychological Thought about Death

In chapter 1, I mentioned a couple of mental tools, describers, that deal with our intuitive, nonreflective beliefs about people. One, the living-thing describer, generates numerous nonreflective beliefs regarding people's biological properties. For instance, as animals, we require food, we sleep, we reproduce young like ourselves, and we die. From the preschool years, at least in predator–prey contexts, people already seem to have a sense that biological processes—needing food, getting tired, moving around—terminate on death. So much becomes a part of our reflexive reasoning about animals. Intuitively, then, we understand what it means when people biologically die.

On the other hand, people exist as psychological or mental creatures as well as biological ones. We think, feel, believe, desire, plan, intend, contemplate, and consider. These same preschoolers (and many adults) who understand that eating, sleeping, and moving end at death do not seem to understand that death terminates mental activities such as thinking and wanting (even considering less cerebral animals). Why the dissociation between biological and psychological activities? Because these two classes of properties get processed through two different mental tools. The living-thing describer tackles biological properties. ToM handles the psychological. Apparently, the living-thing describer builds in the belief that death (a biological event) terminates biological processes, but as a biological event, ToM does not register that death necessarily ends psychological processes. That is, biological death appears to be quite intuitive, whereas psychological death is non- or counterintuitive. The result is a conflict in intuitions.

When someone dies, our living-thing describer tells us that the person will never function biologically again. Our ToM, however, keeps generating predictions about what the deceased thinks, believes, hears, and feels. Such continued production of predictions and inferences may be especially likely when it is someone close to us who has died. Thus, spilling out plausible ideas about the deceased's thoughts and wishes may not be very difficult at all. Accustomed to reasoning about people who are not present, ToM happily continues to suppose the mental states of the deceased. Slips of speech, as when we continue to talk about recently deceased loved ones in the present tense, may be evidence of ToM's blindness to the person's death. "Oh, Bob wouldn't like that. He's doesn't like lilies—er, I mean he didn't like lilies." ToM even more readily continues generating mental states when a corpse is present. Through a lifetime of association between human bodies and mentalistic agency, HADD and ToM respond to a human body (especially a known one) as an agent, even in the absence of normal signs of agency, such as movement.

This dissociation between what the living-thing describer tells us about dead persons (they don't function anymore) and what ToM tells us (they continue to function) automatically makes a dead person a minimally counterintuitive thing and attention demanding. Additionally, that our mind already sees death as a counterintuitive state and assumes that mental activities continue on may make ideas about life continuing after death, as spirit or ghost, very attractive. Relative to other concepts, we would expect ghost and spirit concepts to be easily remembered and readily transmitted. As concepts of ghosts and ancestor spirits easily prey on how our mind, left to its own devices, is inclined to reason about the dead, such concepts also enjoy immediate and powerful intuitive plausibility—even independent of "seeing ghosts" or other HADD experiences.[24] It is no wonder, then, that ghost concepts exist essentially everywhere and in strikingly similar forms.

Imagining What It Is Like to Be Dead

A second possible reason that ghost and spirit concepts are so contagious deals with our ability to imagine what it is like to be dead. As mentioned previously, preschool children and many adults seem to expect the dead to cease all biological functions but not mental functions. Well, it turns out that of the various types of mental states, children and adults have the least confidence about the continuation after death of those mental functions that most directly map on to biological functions. People tend to report that the dead no longer eat and continue to think but perhaps do not feel hungry. The dead no longer look around and continue to know what is around but maybe do not see anything. These mental states that directly concern bodily activities such as feeling hungry or tired, feeling pain, and seeing appear to be intermediate cases for which young children (and adults) have few strong convictions.

The explanation that biological and psychological mental tools work at odds might account for these findings. Perhaps, thought about states such as feeling hungry get generated by two different mental tools that give different nonreflective beliefs about the dead. Consequently, we just don't know what to think.

Here is another possible explanation suggested by psychologist Jesse Bering.[25] One strategy people have and use to predict the mental states of others is called *simulation*. If someone's perspective, belief, desire, or other mental state is not immediately obvious, we may imagine what it would be like to be in the other person's condition. Doing so allows us to simulate what the other might be thinking. We use our own experiences and mental states as a model for another person's. What we think we would think or feel if we were the other person becomes ToM's best guess for that other person's mental states. Typically this process takes place nonconsciously. To illustrate, if I see a child lose a balloon and start crying, putting myself into the child's place I can simulate that I would feel unhappy if I lost a balloon. Hence, I suppose the child feels unhappy because of the lost balloon.

Bering observed that the difficulty with which people have imagining some mental state to terminate at death seems related to how hard it is to imagine those mental states ceasing under other conditions. I know what it is like to stop feeling hungry. After I eat, I don't feel hungry anymore. Thus, I can easily simulate that a dead person does not feel hungry anymore. The same could be said for feeling tired or feeling pain. However, I do not know what it is like to not think anymore. I have never consciously experienced "not thinking," so I have a hard time simulating a dead person as not thinking. Likewise, simulating not feeling, not desiring, and not knowing is not easy.

Bering even suggested that this inability to simulate the end of some mental states provides a nonconscious motivation to believe in life after death, ghosts, or spirits. Because people have a hard time imagining that mental processes stop after death and an easy time imagining that they continue, we tend to believe in ghosts or ancestor spirits.

As ancestor spirits play a central role in the oldest religions, this simple by-product of the way our minds work may go a long way to explaining where religions came from. Consider the following. An ancient person died suddenly, leaving a grieving clan whose minds tell them that the person continues to think, feel, believe, and know. A peculiar event occurs shortly after the person's death that encourages an intentional/social explanation. Perhaps the deceased's chief rival and enemy in the clan has his (and only his) hut struck by lightning—something that has never happened before. Biased toward social explanations for unusual events, someone floats the idea that the deceased person would have wanted that to happen. No other explanation exists for the event. So the people begin musing about the possibility that the dead man perpetrated the act. One woman, sympathetic to the rival, proclaims that if the dead had done it, it was a nasty thing to do. The next day, she (and no one else) falls dreadfully ill. At this point, the whole clan believes (some more confidently than others) that the dead person is still an agent that may act on them, and so they try to stay on his good side. A protoreligion is born.

I am not suggesting that a scenario like this actually gave rise to religion as we know it. What I am suggesting by this illustration is that the sorts of minds we have require little peculiar inputs from the environment in order to rapidly move us toward belief in gods and full-blown religion.

Notes

1. For a fine, brief overview, see Lawson (1985).
2. Katz (2000); Turiel (1998).
3. Henrich and Gil-White (2001).
4. Hirschfeld (1994a, 1994b, 1995).
5. Cosmides and Tooby (1989).
6. Boyer (2001); Lewis (1944).
7. Katz (2000).
8. For a similar argument wholly independent of recent advances in evolutionary behavioral sciences, see Lewis (1944).
9. Boyer (2001).
10. Boyer (2001), chapter 5.
11. Whitehouse (1996a).
12. Knight, Sousa, Barrett, and Atran (in press).
13. Henrich and Gil-White (2001).
14. I do not mean to imply that gods always do act as moral police or that they act consistently. Rather, gods *may* be brought in to moral considerations and be claimed to mete out justice. Consequently, god concepts gain even more attention and more exercise in important and broad areas of human concern.
15. Gilovich (1991).
16. Hacking (1987).
17. For a more developed discussion of the relations between probabilistic reasoning, notions of chance, luck, and divine activity, see Slone (in press).
18. Aronson (1999).
19. Through many experiments, psychologist Leda Cosmides has powerfully demonstrated how easily people negotiate these social contingencies as compared with formally similar problems from nonsocial domains (Cosmides, 1989; Cosmides & Tooby, 1989).

20. Though some gods may be said to behave capriciously or inconsistently with regard to these intuitive principles, these principles remain a benchmark by which the god's behavior may be evaluated. Immoral behavior in gods is possible, as was the case with ancient Greek gods and the Hindu Krishna (at least by some accounts). My contention is that connecting the gods' behavior with moral and social exchange intuitions makes the god more plausible and more intimately connected with human concerns, hence encouraging belief and spread of the god concept.

21. Gods may be wronged in ways that seem very peculiar, as in sacrificing an animal with a trivial blemish or reciting a phrase improperly. Though theologies may develop complex systems for determining what counts as offending the gods, for these theologies to be successfully understood and accepted by the masses, such systems must ultimately fall back on intuitive principles. Comparably, people may register moral indignation at any number of behaviors that seem, at least on the surface, benign. Take, for instance, the idea that women should have their breasts covered by some kind of clothing and that not doing so would be an immoral act. The chain of reasoning that connects such a culturally variable expectation to intuitive moral principles may be long and winding but typically exists nonetheless.

22. Whitehouse (1995) vividly details aspects of the life and religion of the Baining of Papua New Guinea, a traditional society with a religious tradition focused on ancestor spirits.

23. Concerns about death and the afterlife frequently become linked with religious beliefs and the activity of gods (generally speaking) but not necessarily to the primary god or gods of a religious tradition. In traditions featuring ancestor spirits as central characters in the religion, these observations about how the mind deals with death play a large role in explaining how these spirit concepts become commonly believed. In traditions such as Christianity, in which ghosts hold a very peripheral role, the peculiarities of how the human mind deals with death holds little influence on the central deity but may inform beliefs in life after death.

24. Such alleged detections of ghosts may be especially common immediately after someone has died or after a funeral. The salience of the person's death and absence may make otherwise forgettable incidences seem like the dead trying to communicate.

25. Bering (2002).

TO THIS POINT, I have tried to show how belief in gods comes naturally from the way our minds function in the ordinary world, independent of preexisting religious systems and doctrines. The structures of our minds promote the occasional suggestion of unseen agents around us that might have unusual powers or properties, and then our mental tools make the idea of a god or gods memorable, attention demanding, and likely to spread from person to person. Their ability to activate numerous mental tools in various important situations increases the likelihood of these god concepts becoming affirmed as beliefs.

Most of these dynamics would encourage belief in gods even in the absence of others already believing in gods and acting on those beliefs. But people do believe in gods prior to us and do act on those beliefs. Sometimes such beliefs subtly impact personal behavior, as in additional impetus to behave morally, and sometimes such beliefs birth tremendous corporate behavioral displays and commitments of resources, such as Catholic Mass in a spectacularly ornate and enormous cathedral. Religious *actions* further strengthen belief in gods among the believers and also encourage the spread of beliefs to others.

The Importance of Religious Actions Generally

Religious actions, those inspired or shaped by belief in gods, come in various forms, including worship services, prayer, *rituals*, ceremonies of various sorts, acts of charity, meditations, teaching, recitations, reading scriptures, dance, and musical performances. This broad spectrum of religious actions may be performed publicly and corporately or privately and individually. Both public and private religious acts contribute to belief in the gods that motivate their performance.[1]

First, public religious acts may support and encourage belief through pressures of conformity to the group. A public religious act, such as commonly occurs in the places of worship in major religions, gives visual and tangible evidence of others' commitments. It is one thing to say that one believes in a god, but it is quite another to *act* as if one believes in a god. Such evidence of others' commitment becomes part of the corpus of inputs that support reflective belief. Not only do nonreflective beliefs and perhaps some memories and experiences converge on belief in a god, but known and trusted others also testify to the reasonableness of belief in the god.

As a few scholars of religion have begun emphasizing, the power for public religious actions to reinforce belief may increase with the costliness of the behaviors involved.[2] Suppose a group of believers, armed with firearms, comes into a small café and demands that all who believe in their god raise their hands. Well, if the five people in the café raise their hands, such a public act will do little to reinforce the belief of anyone present. The cost of disbelief grossly outweighs belief. On the other hand, if the marauders asking for a hand raise are hostile toward believers and might actually kill them, then the simple act of raising a hand becomes very costly and consequently very convincing to others. Of course, public religious actions in much of the world rarely come in such extreme varieties, but most do carry some costs. Regular attendance at a long and perhaps tedious worship service costs time. Financially supporting the activities of a religious group may be costly. Agreeing to missionary service in faraway and hostile environments qualifies as costly religious behavior. Even publicly acknowledging belief in the face of ridicule counts as a cost. Such public religious actions may all serve to increase the belief of others who witness these displays. But similarly, public religious actions, especially costly ones, serve to reinforce belief in those who *perform* the actions.

Dissonance Reduction

In common thought, attitudes or beliefs drive behaviors, but psychologists have shown that in some situations, behaviors we have performed may change our attitudes or beliefs. The classic theory that explains this dynamic is *cognitive dissonance theory*.[3] In brief, cognitive dissonance theory says that when we act in a way that appears inconsistent with our beliefs, we feel a certain amount of internal dissonance or tension. We seek to resolve this tension by bringing our beliefs in line with our action as performed. For instance, Benjamin Franklin observed that if he got someone to do him a favor, that person would like him more. Sounds backward, doesn't it? The idea is that somewhere in the nonconscious operations of peoples' mind, they reason, "I did Benjamin a favor. Why did I go through the trouble? I must like him better than I thought." The dissonance produced by performing an unwarranted act of kindness gets resolved by a change in attitudes or beliefs so that they better warrant the act. Countless experiments have demonstrated the power of this insight, and many sales and marketing strategies capitalize on it.

Applying cognitive dissonance theory to public religious behaviors, we see how participation may strengthen belief. Suppose Lisa goes to a worship service with her friend even though she has little commitment to the religion. She "suffers" through the experience and—because of a nonconscious desire not to stick out—goes along with all the actions, the singing, the kneeling, the praying, and the responsive readings. Lisa's activities in the face of a lack of commitment to the faith create dissonance. If no explanation (such as pleasing her friend) satisfies this dissonance, her beliefs will move closer in line with her actions, increasing her commitment to the religion.

Allow me to put this belief change in terms of the belief dynamics described in chapter 1. Belief gets built up by an increase in the number of mental tools' outputs converging on the same nonreflective belief. Experiences and memories for one's own behaviors count among these relevant signals for or against belief. If someone acts in a way consistent with belief (even if reflectively they may not believe), an additional piece of data gets added to the belief register; an additional nonreflective reason for belief becomes available: it makes sense of actions performed.

The proselytizing that many religions practice provides a common example of such self-persuasion in religion. When Mormons or Jehovah's Witnesses (to take just two groups famous for this practice) perform door-to-door evangelism, the result is not just piquing the interest of nonbelievers in their faith but also solidifying belief in those doing the evangelism. Going to strangers' homes, getting brushed off, and speaking about one's intimate beliefs typically produce a degree of discomfort and anxiety. These experiences become salient memories and feelings consistent with their religious beliefs and thus add to the number nonreflective systems affirming belief. When attempting to form a reflective belief, more nonreflective reasons weigh in on the side of belief. To put this process back in cognitive dissonance terms, the evangelist (nonconsciously, usually) wonders why he is doing this to himself. The most salient answer is that he must be very committed to his faith. Thus, he becomes more committed and convinces himself of his belief.[4]

Inoculation Effects

In some public religious actions, others may verbally attack one's faith, such as in door-to-door or street-corner evangelism. When this happens, another dynamic may help promote belief. The *inoculation effect* gains its name from its similarity with inoculations against infectious diseases. When a person receives an inoculation, typically a weakened or otherwise inactive form of a virus gets injected. The body's immune system reacts to the intruder, readying it for other, more life-threatening attacks. Likewise, when a belief of ours is mildly challenged by others, we often have resources, such as argumentation, evidence, or social support, that help us counter the attack. Having successfully withstood the challenge of an opponent, our confidence in our belief becomes strengthened. Such a process is the inoculation effect.[5]

In religious contexts, the application is straightforward. Patricia believes in the Trinity. Rif challenges her by saying, "Listen. One being existing as three persons is logically impossible. If you believe in the Father, Son, and Holy Spirit as all being divine, then you are a polytheist." Because Rif's challenge is not severe and maybe is familiar to Patricia, she could already have a defense. Patricia answers, "For a two-dimensional creature, a cube can only have one face. But for a three-dimensional creature, a cube has six-faces. Maybe in our limited understanding a being can only exist as one person, but the Divine may really exist as three persons. I see no logical contradiction."[6] Rif walks away perplexed, and Patricia is emboldened in her Trinitarian belief. She is emboldened because she has added yet another item to the nonreflective belief ledger: a memory of having adequately defended her belief. Nonreflectively, if she were able to defend a belief, the memory of the successful defense would count as evidence that the belief is true.

More Domains of Activity, More Reasons for Belief

Recall the principle that the more mental tools with which an idea fits, the more likely it is to become a (reflective) belief. One of the ways public religious acts subserve belief is by increasing the number of domains or contexts in which belief is exercised. The more contexts, the more mental tools work in consonance with the belief. Rituals and prayers may constitute petitions to get a god to heal, remedy misfortune, mend relationships, change emotional states, bring rain, or encourage reproduction. Similarly, sermons, prophecies, and other teachings may connect the activity of a god to countless domains of human activity and interest. With each proposed advance of divine activity into additional realms of thought and action, the belief in the god becomes more intricately woven into the fabric of the believer's life. Consequently, reflective belief grows even stronger.

Coordinated Religious Actions

Many of the public religious actions I have mentioned thus far amount to individuals acting on their own in a public arena. But many religious events require the coordinated activity of multiple individuals. Corporate singing, dancing, readings, and prayer are examples. Many rituals and ceremonies require more than one actor, such as in weddings or various initiation rites. In addition to serving as demonstrations of commitment, these coordinated events may emphasize unity in belief and reinforce trust in a community. If a believer witnesses another praying, that may serve as testimony of the other's belief; but if two believers pray *together*, they demonstrate to *each other* that they have similar beliefs and can trust each other in those beliefs. Some scholars of religion, emphasizing evolutionary advantages of religion, point to these coordinated religious actions as important builders of cooperation and mutuality. Thus, they argue, by virtue of this behaviorally established trust in comparable value systems, religious communities may show better cooperation than nonreligious ones. Consequently, religious communities (historically) have had a greater likelihood of survival, passing on their religiously cooperative genes.[7]

Contributions of Specific Types of Religious Behaviors to Belief

Ceremonies

Weddings, funerals, worship services, and countless other religious events often take the form of fairly elaborate ceremonies. These events include the actions of numerous individuals acting according to some coordinated structure. Religious ceremonies run the gamut from very emotionally charged, highly ornate affairs, as in many weddings and funerals, to fairly boring, subdued events, as in many weekly worship services. They also range from frequently performed events, such as weekly worship services of many faiths, to fairly infrequently performed ones, such as bar mitzvahs and bas mitzvahs, which a person performs only once in a lifetime, and the Muslim pilgrimage, or hajj, which typically is only performed only once in a Muslim's life. Some cognitive scientists of religion have noticed that the emotionality, or *sensory pageantry*, of religious ceremonies seems to be closely related to their frequency of performance, and these features differentially impact the transmission of ideas and religious belief.[8]

ONE-OFF CEREMONIES Some ceremonies occur (ideally) once for individuals in their lifetimes. Baptisms, circumcisions, weddings, confirmations, ordinations, initiations, and funerals constitute examples of "one-off" ceremonies. Anthropologist Harvey Whitehouse observed that many (if not most) of these infrequently performed ceremonies take highly emotional and dramatized forms. The initiation rites or rites of passage of many cultures may be particularly traumatic and brutal, earning the label "rites of terror."[9] In contrast to the relatively cheerful and celebratory Jewish bar mitzvah, in many Melanesian rites of passage, the men of the village beat, burn, starve, freeze, cut, and otherwise torture prepubescent boys to mark their coming of age. Rites of terror amount to a religious form of hazing. Whitehouse notes that compared to frequently performed ceremonies, these one-off, highly emotional ceremonies typically include very little verbal instruction or teaching about the gods.

How, then, might these ceremonies contribute to the formation of beliefs? Two related factors contribute to these emotional ceremonies powerfully impacting belief: the peculiarity and memorability of them.

These one-off ceremonies powerfully strike participants as unusual, peculiar experiences. The level of emotional arousal through terror, ecstasy, or grief marks these events off from ordinary life. Likewise, the fact that members of one's community—often one's family and loved ones—have gone through tremendous efforts to make this event particularly joyful or terrible makes these events peculiar. These distinctive features of the ceremony make these important and perhaps defining events in the participants' lives. Having minds that perpetually seek to understand why things happen as they do, the peculiarity of these events prompt nonconscious and conscious searching for the *meaning* of the event. Why would my otherwise gentle, loving, and generous father starve, beat, and burn me? Though little verbal explanation for all the hoopla is offered, the experience, complete with fragmentary explanations, distinctive images, sounds, and smells, may provide a lifelong target to be thought about and explained by explicit suggestions that come later at other events or through one's private ruminations.

The high emotional intensity and unusual character makes the experience unforgettable. Contrary to popular notions of "repressed memories" or amnesia in the face of trauma, the truth is that emotional arousal typically improves memory for an event, even to the point of making the memory hauntingly hard to shake. For people who live through events such as a severe natural disaster or a brutal attack, such events most often accurately stay with them in vivid detail for the rest of their lives. Psychologists sometimes refer to these memories for emotional events as "flashbulb memories" because of their vividness many years later. (I should note that this vivid accuracy may apply only to events one has actually experienced firsthand. Hearing about a serious event, such as public figure being assassinated, may also produce a vivid memory, but research has shown such memories to be largely unreliable.)[10] Two aspects of the ceremonies that may be particularly memorable to the participant are the unusual images related to the procedure of the ceremony and the other fellow participants.

In his discussion of the "imagistic mode of religiosity," in which these infrequently performed and highly emotional ceremonies take place, Whitehouse notes that the images incorporated into these ceremonies often include very ordinary items from initiates' lives. He goes on to suggest that these items (such as hair, fur, fat, dew, and taro) tease initiates' imaginations to find connections between religious beliefs and day-to-day life. Reasoning through analogies, such images help them relate their experiences in the ceremony to mundane events of ordinary life. After undergoing such a ceremony, common practices, such as hunting, farming, or eating, take on new, theological importance through the haunting memories of the ceremony.[11] Thus, the reach of theological beliefs expands by participation in the ceremony. More mental tools connect daily activities with theological beliefs, thereby enhancing belief.

These peculiar, memorable religious ceremonies powerfully illustrate the commitment of the community to some set of religious beliefs—beliefs strong enough for them to behave in otherwise inexplicable ways, spending gross amounts of resources on some joyous event, or abusing the most cherished people in their lives. Further, as the fellow participants typically are clearly remembered because of the emotional arousal, a new relational bond may be established between them. The shared traumatic experience binds them together. Together they experienced something horrible or wonderful but certainly bizarre. As in public religious events more generally, a degree of dissonance reduction may be at play here. Unconsciously or even consciously, participants may wonder, "Why did I allow myself (even though I was the 'victim') to go through this ceremony?" The ready answer may be, "It must be important to me to be a part of this community with whom I share *beliefs*." As is the reputed result of surviving a plane crash or the hazing to get into a social club or fraternal organization, the participants in an extreme religious ceremony may find their commitment to the beliefs of the community greatly deepened.[12]

ONE-OFF RITUALS According to cognitive scientists of religion Bob McCauley and Tom Lawson, a religious *ritual*, technically, is a single action.[13] A ritual action involves a person (or agent) performing some act on someone or something else in order to bring about a particular state of affairs that does not naturally follow from the action. So a city mayor cutting a ribbon to officially open a bridge is a ritual. Someone (the mayor) does something (cuts) to someone or something (the ribbon) to bring about some state that does not naturally follow from the action (cutting ribbons does not typically open bridges). A *religious* ritual adds just one other factor: a god must be involved or appealed to in some way. Hence, a woman dabbing water on her own forehead does not amount to a religious ritual. If no god is involved, she simply gets wetter. However, things change if the power of a god somehow is involved in the procedure. For instance, if the water had been previously blessed by a representative of God (a priest, thus imputing it with special power), the simple act becomes a religious ritual.

Many religious ceremonies include at least one and sometimes many religious rituals. A Catholic worship service, for instance, often includes a self-blessing with holy water on entrance of the sanctuary, a blessing-of-the-host ritual, and the actual Mass ritual of consuming the bread and wine. Additionally, the Catholic service may include baptisms, confirmations, and other rituals. Thus, one *ceremony* (the worship service) can involve a large number of individual *rituals*.

Lawson and McCauley observed that, for ceremonies that include a ritual in their technical sense, the degree of emotionality surrounding the ceremony may be fairly accurately predicted on the basis of the type of ritual that holds a central place in the ceremony. Specifically, for rituals in which ordinary people act on or through a god (or representative of the god), the degree of emotionality and sensory pageantry is relatively low. However, for rituals in which a representative of the god does the acting, sensory pageantry becomes heightened. To illustrate, a Catholic Mass (that is, a worship service centering around the ritual of consuming the bread and wine) has relatively low sensory pageantry as compared with a typical Catholic wedding. Why so? In the Mass, ordinary people act on the god when parishioners eat the bread and wine representing Jesus (God). In the wedding, a representative of God (the priest) acts on two ordinary people to make them one new entity "in the sight of God." McCauley and Lawson note that this pattern seems to recur across religious systems. Rituals in which the god, usually through a representative, does the acting are relatively high in sensory pageantry and emotionality. Cross-religiously recurrent examples are weddings, funerals, rites of passage, initiations, and ordinations. Note that, similar to Whitehouse's observation, the rituals in which the gods do the acting are one-off rituals that a person participates in (usually) only once in a lifetime. Rituals in which the god is acted on by ordinary people tend to be lower in emotionality and sensory pageantry. Examples include sacrifices of various sorts, ritual blessings, and ritual cleansings. A single person often performs the same rituals multiple times.

Lawson and McCauley explain this pattern through a series of cognitive mechanisms whose functioning lies beyond the scope of the present discussion.[14] What is relevant here about their theory is the observation that the heightened sensory pageantry and resulting emotionality of one-off rituals may serve to impress on the participants in the ritual and observers that a real change is happening to them. When the gods act, you *feel* it. Their action fills up the senses and floods us with emotions. The pomp and circumstance—the sounds, lights, colors, and aromas—of the wedding boldly announce, especially to the bride and groom, that something of profound importance is taking place. A god is acting to change the status of these two people once and for all. The happy couple *feel* the activity of the god.

If McCauley and Lawson correctly assess the typical dynamics of one-off rituals, then these rituals play a special role in reinforcing belief in the deity. As with other rituals and ceremonies, belief is reinforced because of the public demonstration of belief in the god producing social pressure, testimony of others, and self-convincing dynamics, all of which encourage belief. But additionally, the often-intense emotional experience may make the god's presence felt in such a way that the hypersensitive agency detection device (HADD) screams that the god is acting. Anchoring such a profound personal experience with this experience of the god's activity gives the participant a long-lasting memory that assures one of the reality of the deity.

Repeated Ceremonies

Whitehouse has also observed that frequently repeated religious ceremonies, whether or not they include rituals, typically have relatively low sensory pageantry or emotionality. Compare, for instance, a typical Methodist or Lutheran worship service with a typical Methodist or Lutheran wedding or funeral. The worship service pales in comparison. It might even be downright boring. Unlike their one-off counterparts, these repeated ceremonies usually involve a fair amount of verbal communication in the form of readings or sermons. It is in these contexts, termed the "doctrinal mode of religiosity,"[15] that a different sort of belief development takes place.

Whereas the highly emotive, one-off rituals and ceremonies create emotions and impressions that encourage rumination about the activity of the gods, the more somber, repetitive gatherings provide occasion to verbally discuss beliefs and provide explicit reasons for belief. Take Christian sermonizing, for instance. Christian theology may sometimes be quite counterintuitive, far more complex than the optimal "minimally counterintuitive" concepts discussed in chapter 2. Explaining how it is that God is outside of time (nontemporal) and how this characteristic makes God able to know our futures without compromising either God's sovereignty or our free will is not the banal material our mental tools handle with ease. Rather, such theologizing requires careful, verbal explanation and repetitive presentation to ensure uniform orthodoxy among believers. Religions with such complicated theologies, then, require occasions to repetitively present doctrinal positions. Repeated ceremonies afford such occasions to systematically and logically (assuming certain belief premises) present reasons for these complex theological beliefs.

Those who work in the persuasion and propaganda fields, such as advertising, know the power of proclamation. When people hear similar claims repeatedly, even though they receive no evidence or proper justification for the claim, they tend to believe the claim. The more familiar the claim, the more intuitively true it seems. Thus, someone who hears the truth of the Divine Trinity affirmed weekly for years will tend to accept its truth, even if no strong evidence or justification has ever been offered.

Repeated ceremonies also offer multiple opportunities to explicitly draw out the implications of theological claims. For instance, consider the following argument:

> If God designed the world and humans, then God knows what is best for us.
> If God is loving, we can trust that God asks us to do what is best for us.
> Therefore, we should do as God asks of us.
> Hence, if God tells us to rest one of every seven days, we should do so.

Such theological reasoning is not necessarily transparent to everyone and may need to be made explicit several times at regular intervals before it is understood, let alone believed. Further, connecting basic theological premises (such as God-as-creator or God-as-loving) to real life activities encourages the inclusion of God (or gods) in many different domains of thought on a day-to-day basis. The more different domains in which religious thought is integrated, the more mental tools become confident in their nonreflective beliefs in God and consequently the stronger reflective belief in God becomes.

Some Additional Observations Concerning Ritual and Prayer

Gods receive numerous petitions for aid of various sorts. These petitions may come by way of prayers or rituals. According to Lawson and McCauley, rituals differ from prayer in that a correctly performed religious ritual *guarantees* the desired outcomes. If one properly performs a ritual to bring rain, rain will come. In contrast, a prayer requesting rain may or may not bring rain, depending on the whims of the deity being petitioned. If a ritual fails, believers question the qualifications of those who conducted the ritual, the quality of the materials used, or the required state of mind of those involved. They do not doubt the ability of the god to deliver and certainly not the god's existence. If a petitionary prayer fails to achieve desired results, the faith of the one who prayed may be questioned, but just as likely to be doubted is the legitimacy or appropriateness of the request or the motivation of the god to deliver. Just as a parent might inexplicably deny a request, so might a god inexplicably deny a prayer request. Believers do not doubt the power or existence of the god. But why don't failed petitions, either through ritual or prayer, shake the faith of believers?

Concerning religious rituals, McCauley and Lawson observe that religious systems that have staying power exercise only those rituals over which they have a large degree of "conceptual control." By conceptual control, these scholars refer precisely to a ritual's ability to withstand alleged evidence of failure. For instance, a religion that has a ritual that guarantees to change all men purple exactly ten seconds after the ritual's completion would not last long—at least this ritual would not. Evidence of its failure would be obvious and hard to explain away. The purple-men-maker ritual would have poor "conceptual control." McCauley and Lawson specifically use the example of a series of rituals performed by a splinter group of people in Papua New Guinea, reported by Whitehouse.[16] These rituals guaranteed that the ancestor spirits would return immediately. When the ancestors did not return, the splinter group tried again and again but ultimately returned to the mainstream religion of the community. Their rituals had poor conceptual control.

Common religions around the world use a number of rituals with strong conceptual control. Baptisms, which result in the forgiveness of sins or membership in a community of "saved" people, cannot be easily falsified. Likewise, weddings that mystically join two people can be reversed (through divorce), but the ritual does not fail when performed properly.

I do not mean to suggest that religious leaders deliberately set forth to dupe the masses by using only carefully concocted religious rituals that resist falsification well. Rather, the religious rituals (and traditions) that survive will be those that do not have rituals obviously fail. A selective process is at play. Religious rituals and related religious systems that are most obviously false or that cannot withstand confrontations with advances in philosophy and science will be most readily abandoned.

I suspect that the relative success of religions such as Christianity and Islam, the two largest religions in the world, have to do with their use of rituals that have extremely strong conceptual control. Unlike many traditional religions still practiced in parts of Africa, Australia, and Asia, the rituals of Christianity and Islam typically do not try to address practical problems, such as bringing rain, ensuring fertility, or healing sickness. This not only protects them against technological advances such as in medicine but also provides philosophical and scientific skeptics little room to disagree with the consequences of the rituals.[17] Again, I am not suggesting that this protection is devious and deliberate.

Petitionary prayer might be said to have strong conceptual control as well. As I mentioned previously, prayer commonly assumes the possibility that a request could be approved, denied, or put off until a later date. If one asks a god to heal someone and the healing does not come until months later, the prayer could still be understood as having been granted, just on a different timetable than anticipated. Or if the healing never comes, perhaps the god denied the request for any one of a number of reasons. As in making requests of another person, the answer is not always "yes." Hence, a prayer that is not obviously answered does not necessarily threaten belief. I know that if I were a superknowledgeable god, I wouldn't let mere mortals coerce me into doing nearsighted or silly things through religious rituals or prayers. I would keep my own counsel.

The ability of prayer to withstand skeptical scrutiny gains further strength from the sorts of things that believers often request. Recent studies of prayer behaviors of Christians, Muslims, and Jews suggest a tendency to ask for the deity to act primarily in either the psychological realm (for example, to change minds, affect emotional states, or influence relationships) or in areas that involve unclear causal mechanisms (as in having "good fortune"). The studies show that believers do not frequently pray for God to act in ways that obviously violate normal biological or mechanical processes.[18]

Clear evidence that prayed requests and religious rituals with adequate conceptual control have failed cannot easily be mustered. The ritual may have worked (and we just can't tell), or it did fail because of performance problems. The prayer may have been declined, or perhaps the answer was "not now." Thus, negative evidence rarely threatens belief in gods. On the other hand, when rituals or prayers do "work," the positive results may be powerfully salient and hard to explain (convincingly) in other terms.

A friend of mine named Frank once had a horse roll over on him, shattering his leg. Bone marrow got into his bloodstream, causing deadly clots. After several days of futile treatment, doctors gave up and summoned Frank's family members to come and say good-bye. The blood clots would kill him within the day. Frank, not previously a "true believer," asked for God's help. That night, he felt a warmth rush over his body and a feeling of peace and confidence that his request was granted. In the morning, he tried to reassure his family and medical staff that he was not going to die. To humor him, doctors consented to running further tests, and miraculously all blood clots were completely gone. Frank was fully healed.

For Frank, his family members, and others involved with his story, the most intuitively plausible explanation was that his prayer was indeed answered affirmatively. Though other, biochemical explanations might be available, their utter complexity and exceptionality would render them fairly weak as an attack against the sort of belief in divine activity this event prompted. Such positive evidence of a god strongly supports belief. Negative evidence, because it is often intuitively weak, offers little challenge to belief. On the whole, then, petitionary prayer and religious rituals (with adequate conceptual control) offer more opportunity to support than undermine belief.

Minimally Counterintuitive Rituals

Though my purpose here is not to explain where religious ceremonies, rituals, and prayer come from, I want to make one comment regarding the plausibility of rituals. Many religious rituals, and prayer for that matter, gain much of their intuitive plausibility through analogy with well-known behavioral processes. Often religious rituals may be said to resemble ordinary actions. For instance, many ritual cleansings appearing in traditions around the world suggest the more natural forms of bathing. Some approximations come closer to the genuine article (as in Baptist immersion baptism) than others (such as Catholic sprinkling baptism), but they approximate the source of the analogy closely enough that the target ritual may be easily understood. For a religious authority to claim that a ritual cleansing washes away spiritual impurities much as how a physical bath washes away physical impurities strikes ordinary folk as more intuitively plausible than claiming that performing some completely arbitrary set of actions would result in spiritual purity. Akin to how minimally counterintuitive concepts enjoy a selective advantage over wildly counterintuitive ones or painfully common ones, minimally counterintuitive rituals may be memorable and possess certain intuitiveness.

Once a set of fairly plausible rituals, ceremonies, and prayer practices become established in a community, they may serve to promote religious belief in the many ways described in this chapter. By acting "as if" we believe particular religious claims and their implications, we come to believe them more strongly. Religious actions of various sorts provide these opportunities. Religious actions also provide opportunities to implicitly impress the power of the gods on others or to explicitly argue for belief in gods. Thus, through various means, religious actions encourage the spread of religious beliefs.

Notes

1. I am not attempting to explain why people begin performing religious rituals in the first place. Rather, once rituals and other religious actions have started, they have consequences for encouraging religious belief that may (but need not) then strengthen participation. For more on why people perform religious actions, see Boyer (2001), Lawson and McCauley (1990), McCauley and Lawson (2002), and Whitehouse (2000, 2004).

2. See, for instance, Atran (2002).

3. This theory was developed by Festinger (1957). See also Festinger and Carlsmith (1959).

4. Work on cognitive dissonance has suggested something of an optimum. If dissonance is too great, for instance, if the cost of the religious involvement is enormous, the dissonance might not be easily resolved and persist. Such strong dissonance would challenge religious commitment. If dissonance is too slight, it might produce no attitude change. Returning to the missionary practices of Jehovah's Witnesses, typically an older, more confident and more committed member of the faith goes door to door with a younger member. The younger member does the talking, producing dissonance, but the elder is available to modulate anxiety and head off any greater-than-desired attacks on the faith. These observations apply similarly to inoculation effects (discussed later in this chapter).

5. McGuire (1964). Bateson (1975) showed that religious believers could have their commitment intensified through attacks on their beliefs.

6. This example is taken from Lewis's (1952) far more sophisticated and elegant argument showing that the notion of the Trinity or a hyperperson is not illogical or impossible.

7. Atran (2002) comments on the striking degree of social coordination seen in religious activity and argues that this, among other factors, has provided individual evolutionary advantages for religious activity. Wilson (2002) makes a comparable group-selectionist argument for religion as a social phenomenon.

8. Whitehouse (1995, 1996b, 2000, 2004), Lawson and McCauley (1990), and McCauley and Lawson (2002) have had much to say about the relationship between frequency of performance of religious events and their emotionality. "Sensory pageantry" is a term coined by McCauley and Lawson (2002). Strictly speaking, what I refer to as ceremonies aligns more closely with Whitehouse's use of the term "ritual" than McCauley and Lawson's much more restricted sense of the term.

9. See Whitehouse (1996b, 2000, 2004). For particularly chilling examples of a "rites of terror," see Barth's (1975) descriptions of Baktaman initiations.

10. Whitehouse (2000) says much more about these sorts of memories. For psychological treatments of flashbulb memories, see Brown and Kulik (1982), Neisser and Harsch (1992), and Neisser, Winograd, Bergman, Schreiber, Palmer, and Weldon (1996).

11. See Whitehouse (1996b, 2000).

12. Whitehouse ambitiously argues that numerous sociopolitical consequences follow from these traumatic one-off rituals and their psychological effects. For instance, their special bond with coinitiates especially leads to the formation of a tight-knit, fairly egalitarian community of believers. Further, such religious commitments typically spread very slowly because of the centrality of ritual participation (in contrast, say, to certain theological beliefs). Whitehouse (2000, 2004) terms the clustering of these and other effects the "imagistic mode" of religiosity and contrasts it with the "doctrinal mode," which is characterized by repetitive rituals, emphasis on verbal transmission and argumentation, hierarchical organization, potential for rapid spread, and so forth. Whitehouse's "modes of religiosity" theory thus bridges cognitive and social dynamics in religious systems while remaining empirically testable and comparatively useful.

13. Lawson and McCauley (1990); McCauley and Lawson (2002).

14. For details, see McCauley and Lawson (2002). For a presentation of empirical work concerning the theory, see Barrett (2003).

15. Whitehouse (2000, 2004).

16. McCauley and Lawson (2002); Whitehouse (1995).

17. I consider many tribal religious actions dealing with technical outcomes "endangered" by modern philosophy, science, and technology.

18. Barrett (2001).

The Naturalness of Belief in God   6

TO THIS POINT, it may seem that the cognitive science of religion accommodates all religions in the same manner; one religion is just like any other. Indeed, for very good scientific reasons, emphasizing cross-religion similarities is the way the science of religion is typically done. However, for very bad political reasons, scientific scholars of religion often ignore the differences between religions. Not all religions are created equal.

Assuming that all religions are the same—all equally profitable or costly, equally rational or irrational, and equally well supported by natural mental structures and processes—insulates observers from having to evaluate religions in their own right. A believer of a particular religion may write off the rest as equally worthless, and a nonbeliever may shun them all. But just as the philosophy of religion has shown that not all theologies are equally coherent, not all religions are equally supported and encouraged by human minds in the natural world.

Some religions are like rats and rabbits—fast-breeding, adaptable animals that suffer no danger of extinction. Other religions compare with koalas and California condors—slow-breeding animals requiring fairly special ecological conditions and threatened with extinction.

In this chapter, I argue the somewhat controversial position that many basic aspects of Christian, Jewish, and Muslim theologies give these religions further advantages over some others.[1] These theologies, particularly Islam and Christianity, compare with rats and rabbits. Though including theological concepts that may have arrived relatively late in human history, their worldwide prominence and likely resilience against suppression efforts come (at least in part) from an unusually strong relationship with ordinary mental tools.

Horizontal versus Vertical Transmission

The transmission or spread of ideas and beliefs may be described as either horizontal or vertical. Horizontal transmission refers to beliefs or ideas moving from person to person within a generation. Thus, if I tell my wife a funny joke I heard and she tells it to her coworkers, the joke has spread horizontally. Vertical transmission entails passing on a belief or idea to subsequent generations. I teach my children about world history much the same way I was taught world history by my elders, and so I vertically transmit history to a new generation.

To this point, I have emphasized factors that contribute primarily to the horizontal spread of beliefs in gods. Such an account might explain why people tend to believe in gods and perhaps where beliefs in gods come from but says little about why beliefs continue as a generation of believers ages and passes on. But one of the striking marks of religious beliefs is how they remain relatively constant over vast numbers of generations. For much of this chapter, I now turn more deliberately to factors impacting vertical transmission.

Children Learning about God

The facility with which young children acquire and use god concepts is obvious. Much as in reasoning about other people, children from religious families easily form inferences, explanations, and predictions about gods' mind and behavior in novel and sometimes personal ways. From where does this religious fluency come? Part of the answer certainly lies in exposure to religious thought and action. Though some parents may carefully indoctrinate their children and threaten grave repercussions for disbelief, most religious belief in childhood seems to be more simply absorbed. Children believe because their parents (and other trusted adults) act as if they believe and talk as if they believe. Until given strong reason to believe otherwise, this testimony is powerful.

But such an account of vertical transmission would be overly simplistic if we did not consider the character of the beliefs being transmitted and how well they are accommodated by children's minds. Anyone who has taught children, as either a parent or a teacher, knows full well that children cannot be easily taught just anything. Some ideas seem to stick better than others. Thus, the question to be answered is, Why are many religious ideas so easy for children to adopt?

The Anthropomorphism Hypothesis

One answer to this question has been at the theoretical center of the scientific study of religion and especially in the psychology of religion for over a century. The answer might be called the "anthropomorphism hypothesis." Children learn about people (including their minds and behaviors) and then analogically reason about gods. God concepts amount to taking a representation of humanness and projecting it onto "God" or the gods of any given religion.

The anthropomorphism hypothesis asserts that children merely conceptualize God in the same way that they conceptualize humans, and through development God looks less and less like a human. God begins as a big person living in the sky and then becomes (for many Abrahamic theists) an all-present, formless, unchanging, nontemporal, all-knowing, and all-powerful being. Crude, physical anthropomorphism gives way to God as an abstract being with unusual properties.

An Alternative Answer

In contrast to the anthropomorphism hypothesis, I argue that early-developing mental tools (such as the Theory of Mind [ToM]) are *not* specifically for representing humans and, in fact, actually facilitate the acquisition and use of many features of God concepts of the Abrahamic monotheisms. My contention is that children may easily form representations of God because the relevant underlying mental tools used for thinking about God have two favorable properties. First, rather than being dedicated solely to informing understandings of humans, ToM operates generally on any and all intentional agents. As such, ToM is quite capable of representing humans as well as any other intentional being, from God to ghosts to gorillas. ToM is flexible with regard to many properties that theologies teach that God (but not humans) possesses. Consequently, at least for children, many supernatural properties do not impose undue conceptual burdens.

A second feature of ToM in childhood is that it assumes that many superhuman properties are the norm simply by default. For example, when the hypersensitive agency detection device (HADD) identifies something as an intentional agent, a three-year-old's ToM automatically assumes that the agent has the superhuman property of infallible beliefs (at least under certain parameters discussed later in this chapter). Developmental psychologists continue to find evidence that the godly properties of infallible beliefs, superknowledge, superperception, creative power, and immortality are quite intuitive, at least for young children. Concepts of God are easily accommodated because they play on many of these default assumptions rather than violate them.[2]

God as Superknowing

Over the past fifteen years, one of the most productive areas of cognitive developmental psychology has been the subfield often referred to as "theory of mind," which concerns the mental tool I have been calling by the acronym ToM. This domain of conceptual development concerns how children come to predict and explain human action in terms of mental states, such as percepts, beliefs, and desires. When do children understand that people act so as to satisfy their desires? That beliefs regulate desires? That perception helps form belief? How do children come to this understanding? One of the latest turns in the theory-of-mind subfield has been concern over how children come to understand nonhuman minds, such as those of animals and gods. Some of this research bears directly on the question of whether children mentally represent God through anthropomorphism or whether they have a more general understanding of minds that may actually be biased to successfully represent God's mind as it is understood by the Abrahamic monotheisms and some other traditions.

A well-documented and broadly accepted conclusion from work on ToM is that most children younger than four years old have difficulty understanding beliefs as potentially false or differing from person to person. By age five, most children understand that people may believe something that is not true or have false beliefs.[3] To illustrate, an experimenter presents a young three-year-old with an ordinary cardboard soda-cracker box. The experimenter asks the child (familiar with such crackers) the contents of the box. The child answers that crackers are inside the box. The experimenter then shows the three-year-old that the box actually contains rocks and then recloses the box. After showing the rocks, the experimenter asks the child to suppose his mother enters the room and sees the closed cracker box for the first time. What would she think is inside the box? Most three-year-olds answer "rocks" to this question, indicating they do not appreciate that their mother would be fooled by the appearance of the box and thus form a false belief. In contrast, by age five, most children successfully understand that their mother may have a false belief regarding the contents of the box and assume that there are crackers in the box. Using tasks such as this one and a number of others, developmental psychologists have shown that children seem to progress from assuming that everyone's beliefs are the same as the child's understanding of reality to understanding that beliefs are representations of what *might* be the case. In other words, they begin with a default assumption that beliefs are infallible and must then learn that beliefs can be wrong.

How does this developmental story apply to children's understanding of God? If the anthropomorphism hypothesis is correct, it suggests that children begin by assuming that God's beliefs are infallible just like their mothers' and shift to claiming that God's beliefs are fallible just like their mothers'. Continuing along this line, children will be compelled to move from a "theologically accurate" understanding of God's beliefs to an "inaccurate" one and back again as they age. But this is not what has been found.

Colleagues and I tested this hypothesis using the cracker box task described previously.[4] We presented three- to six-year-old American Protestant children with the rock-containing cracker box. As in previous theory-of-mind research, most three- and four-year-olds answered that their mothers would think "rocks" were in the box, suggesting that they did not yet understand that Mom could entertain incorrect beliefs. Nearly all five- and six-year-old children answered "crackers," knowing that Mom would be fooled by the appearance of the box. However, when asked what God would think was in the box, children at all ages were equally likely to answer "rocks," appreciating that God would not be fooled by the appearance of the box. None of the three-year-olds and only one of the nine six-year-olds said that God would think there were crackers in the box. Collaborators of mine conducted a similar, culture-appropriate task with Maya children in southern Mexico and discovered comparable results. Not only did children seem to reason differently (and more accurately in theological terms) about God than their mothers, but they also reasoned differently about God and other gods and spirits who the Maya do not suppose are all-knowing.[5]

Thus, when reasoning about beliefs, a clear divergence in developmental patterns emerged between children's reports of Mom's beliefs and God's beliefs. In reporting Mom's beliefs, children developed from attributing belief that there were rocks in the box to the false belief that there were crackers in the box. But when reporting God's beliefs, children consistently reported that God would believe there were rocks in the box. Contrary to the anthropomorphism hypothesis, children do not appear compelled to anthropomorphize along this dimension, nor must they move from "theologically accurate" to "theologically inaccurate." Rather, children appeared to be theologically accurate from the first and did not lose this ability.

A similar line of research examining children's assumptions about others' previous knowledge of unfamiliar displays revealed a similar pattern.[6] First, before age five, children seemed biased to overextend who might have pertinent knowledge. Second, three-year-olds more accurately reasoned about their mothers than about God (theologically speaking). Through development, they had to mature to the point of answering correctly for a person but needed only to maintain their naive default assumption to answer correctly for God. Additionally, these studies revealed that even the youngest children successfully discriminated between agents, not merely treating all minds as the same. Three-year-olds answered significantly differently for God and a dog, replying that God but not the dog would know the character of the hidden displays. Similarly, when the three- and four-year-olds were given the prerequisite information for interpreting the displays, they tended to revise their assessment of their mothers' knowledge, perhaps using an "if I know it, mom knows it" strategy. Only three-year-olds, however, significantly revised their estimates of what the dog knew in the face of being given more information about displays. At no age did the children significantly revise their estimate of God's knowledge. It seems that, contrary to the anthropomorphism hypothesis, children began discriminating between agents along this dimension of knowledge even before they possessed a robust understanding of prerequisite knowledge for interpreting visual displays.[7]

The tendency for kids to overestimate what others know makes children quite receptive to the idea of a superknowing God. Being superknowing or infallible seems to be a default assumption that must be outgrown. Thus, this bias may help children rapidly adopt concepts of gods with superknowledge (as opposed to those with not so much knowledge). But this facility does not apply only to children.

Though in development we spend a lot of energy learning when others know what we know or have information that we would like or don't know what we know, we often remain quite poor at these judgments. Even in adulthood we tend to overestimate (or underestimate) what others know. Why? Primarily because of computational simplicity. To know whether someone knows something, we often have to figure out whether that person might have had the relevant experiences to acquire this knowledge. Generally, such computations are cumbersome or impossible. To remedy this problem, we simplify to an all-or-nothing proposition. We assume that others know all that we know (in a particular area) unless we have strong reasons to believe otherwise. Thus, all knowledge we have that is of the mundane sort we intuitively believe others have. However, if some bit of knowledge was hard for us to come by or we acquired only recently, we may actually make the alternative (simple) assumption that others do not have it. This all-or-nothing kind of strategy works well in most situations. As long as we are dealing with people who are like us and have had similar experiences to ours, it fairly accurately predicts others' knowledge. Until the past few centuries, fairly homogenous communities were the rule, and so such a strategy may have been quite accurate throughout the bulk of human existence. Today this heuristic leads to awkward social interactions as when we assume others know what we are talking about when they don't or when we tediously explain to another things they already know quite well.

The upshot of an all-or-nothing strategy for adult reasoning about God is that we find thinking about God as superknowing or infallible rather easy. Consequently, people may find understanding and believing in God as superknowing easier than understanding and believing in a god as only knowing certain things in certain times and places.

I describe God here as superknowing or infallible instead of "omniscient" because it is unlikely that children, or adults for that matter, can truly think about God as knowing absolutely everything. Wrapping our minds around what it might mean to know absolutely everything is not easy or practical. By saying God knows everything, I believe we actually mean that for everything we care to consider whether God knows, God does. We also mean that God is never mistaken, hence infallible.

God as Superperceiving

Another aspect of understanding minds that has been thoroughly investigated is the nature of perception. Research has revealed a developmental progression quite similar to understanding false beliefs. Three-year-olds often have difficulty understanding that just because they see something a certain way, not anyone or everyone else sees it the same way. Consequently, they might mistakenly assume that the book page that appears right side up to them also appears right side up to their mothers, for whom it is actually upside down. By age five, children's ability to appreciate another's visual perspective approximates that of adults. Such a developmental course invites another examination of God concepts along the same dimension.

In one experiment conducted by developmental psychologist Rebekah Richert,[8] children ages three to eight looked through the slit in the top of a darkened shoe box and were asked, "What do you see inside the box?" After the children reported seeing nothing, the experimenter shined the flashlight through a hole, revealing a wooden block inside. Turning off the light, the experimenter then invited the child to look again. Then the experimenter told the child that cats can see in the dark because of their special eyes. Then the experimenter asked the child what a human puppet, a cat puppet, a monkey puppet, and God saw in the darkened box. While most three-year-olds reported that the human puppet could see the block in the darkened box (which had been invisible to themselves), a minority of five-year-olds did so. In contrast, children's answers for God and the cat puppet were importantly different from their answers for either the human puppet or the monkey puppet. A comparable large majority of the three- and five-year-olds answered that God and the cat would see the block—as high as 90 percent in some cases. Once again, even young children embraced decidedly different properties for God as compared with humans. Thus, children's agent concepts supported by ToM appear flexible enough to accommodate superhuman properties.

A second set of studies by Richert, investigating children's understanding of seeing, hearing, and smelling, support these findings.[9] Results revealed that preschoolers may differentiate between various agents when predicting various perceptual experiences. Once again, as with the cracker box task, the previous knowledge tasks, and the darkened box task, as soon as children began to demonstrate understanding of a particular dimension of human minds, they likewise showed discrimination regarding to which minds that dimension applies and readily applied superhuman properties to God. They did not exhibit the wholesale anthropomorphism predicted by the anthropomorphism hypothesis.

God as Immortal

In chapter 4, I mentioned some recent studies of children's and adults' understanding of death. These studies show that, at least when reasoning about animals that have been killed, preschoolers have surprisingly clear notions about the biological consequences of death, but adults and children seem to have much harder times seeing death as the termination of psychological activities. I argued that the way children (and adults) intuitively reason about death contributes to life-after-death ideas and the notion of ghosts and spirits. What we still know fairly little about is whether children understand development, aging, and death as *inevitable* processes. Short of being killed by a violent act, do children understand that people but not gods will eventually die?

Unlike children's understanding of minds, children's understanding of mortality has received relatively little attention, especially God's mortality. One complicating factor in examining children's understanding of God's mortality/immortality in the traditionally Christian world is the salience of the Incarnation. Christianity holds that God was born and did die in the person of Jesus of Nazareth, and this story is reiterated annually at Christmastime. Thus, the theological claim that the Christian God is immortal could be especially difficult for children in such a cultural context. Nevertheless, at least one recent study has explored children's understanding of God's immortality and yielded results consonant with the other findings presented here regarding their strong ability to reason about divine properties.

Developmental psychologist Marta Gimenez and collaborators asked Spanish three- to five-year-olds questions regarding the mortality of a friend versus God's mortality.[10] These questions concerned whether God or their friends were alive at the time of dinosaurs, were ever babies, would grow old, and would die. Answers were compiled for a mortality score. Not unlike in the cracker box task, three-year-olds did not distinguish between a friend and God. Children did not clearly grant mortality to either being. But by age five, children uniformly and accurately attributed mortality to a friend but not to God, for instance, regarding a friend as more likely to age and die than God. Children showed no age-related change in attributing mortality to God, and four- and five-year-olds ascribed mortality to their friends significantly more often than to God. Thus, the anthropomorphism hypothesis failed.

But was there evidence that children were especially receptive to understanding God as immortal? The results were not clear but suggestive. As noted previously, the Incarnation complicates measuring the understanding of immortality, especially when one fourth of the mortality score was based on whether God was ever a baby. It is not at all unreasonable for a Christian child or a child in a Christianized culture to answer that a long time ago God was born as a baby. That is what they are taught every December. Placing this concern aside, the data are still promising. Three-year-olds showed no evidence of entering the task with a default assumption that God and people are mortal; rather, immortality appears to be just as natural an assumption. These young children also tended in the direction of embracing God's immortality more eagerly that their friends' mortality. Perhaps in a predominantly Muslim or Jewish nation where the salience of an incarnational deity is not so strong, ambiguity in questioning children about God's birth and death would be reduced.

Though the body of research is still thin concerning children's understanding of God's immortality versus the mortality of people, available data are consistent with the other research presented earlier. Preschool-aged children need not anthropomorphize God with regard to mortality and, if anything, seem biased to overextend immortality. That is, children may have an early bias to represent intentional agents as immortal. And why not? The inevitability of biological death through natural causes (as opposed to violent ones) may not be obvious in the day-to-day life of most children. Indeed, it seems that even into adolescence, it is children's lack of appreciation of their own mortality that keeps parents on their toes.

God as Superpowerful

Jean Piaget, arguably the most influential developmental psychologist of the twentieth century, advanced the anthropomorphism hypothesis as applied to children's reasoning about God.[11] Piaget's discussion of God concepts drew from two primary observations. First, Piaget noted that many children seven years old or younger seemed to believe that the natural world had been created by human beings. He termed this phenomenon "childhood artificialism." In his interviews, children reported that lakes, clouds, rocks, and other natural things were both younger than humanity and created by humans. Second, Piaget believed that children younger than about seven years old endow their parents and other adults with the properties of omniscience and omnipotence. Through his interviews, repeatedly Piaget found that children believed that adults possessed superpowers that enabled them not only to create mountains and lakes but also to do countless other feats of strength and might. Additionally, Piaget cited the "crisis" that children reportedly face when they find that some things are outside their parents' control or knowledge. Until children outgrow this stage and begin to appreciate human fallibility, God is just another human who just happens to live in the sky. After children understand that humans do not, in fact, possess Godlike properties, God is left as the only member of the pantheon. God is thus a residual of childhood naïveté supported by theological instruction.

Though Piaget underestimated the sophistication of children's ability to think about God and other nonhuman agents, to date I am aware of no evidence that challenges Piaget's observation that young children assume adults have superpowers. Indeed, on this point, it seems likely that Piaget was correct. Children assume that *all* agents, including God and their parents, have superpowers and then pare back parents' abilities as they discover human limitations. Thus, as with understanding God's mental abilities and immortality, young children seem to understand God more accurately than people. They must learn where human limitations of power lie but simplistically allow for God's omnipotence.

God as a Creator

Piaget's version of the anthropomorphism hypothesis was inspired largely by his discovery of "childhood artificialism," the notion that the natural world was created by people. If people can create natural things such as animals, lakes, and rocks, then God doing so places God's power on par with that of humans, and so it is not something special. However, newer investigations have questioned the prevalence of artificialism and suggest that very young children can understand God as distinct from humans in creative capability.

For example, psychologist Olivera Petrovich presented British preschool children with pairs of photographs of various objects such as animals (a dog), plants (daffodils), other natural things (snow and leaves), toy animals and plants, and common artifacts (chair and books).[12] The experimenter asked the children whether either of the two photographs was something that could be made by people. When the pair included a clearly natural thing (such as a leaf) in contrast with an artifact (such as a bus), nearly always children accurately answered which one could be made by people. Only when the pair contained an artificial imitation of a natural kind (such as a toy cow) did children seem to be confused. On the basis of these and other data, Petrovich concluded that when considering origins, preschoolers clearly discriminate between the natural world and the artificial.

In another set of studies, Petrovich connected children's understanding of origins more closely to their concepts of God.[13] British preschoolers answered questions regarding the first origins of either plants, animals, or natural things such as the sky, earth, and large rocks—the same sorts of things Piaget asked about. Given three options—that the things were made by people, made by God, or no one knows—preschoolers were nearly seven times more likely to answer that God was the source of the natural world than people. Taken with the finding that children clearly dismissed the possibility that natural things are made by people, these results seem to suggest that preschoolers may indeed understand God as possessing importantly different creative power than people.

Petrovich's studies undermine the strength of childhood artificialism and provide strong evidence that four-year-old children are capable of representing God as having nonanthropomorphic power. The early age at which children have this capability suggests the ease with which their mental tools invite God to be the cause of natural things. Piaget's fundamental observation that young children are biased to overestimate the power of adults has not been challenged. Perhaps we have good reason to believe that children have a default tendency to represent intentional agents—gods or people—as being superpowerful. What has been challenged is that this superpower bias is a distinctively and indiscriminately human attribute that then gets extended to other agents. It now appears that preschool children can successfully "turn off" the bias when considering the role of humans in origins of the natural world and extend superpowers only to God.

Other studies support the notion that children may have strong dispositions to understand the world as created but not created by humans. Developmental psychologist E. Margaret Evans examined explanations of the origins of things given by five- to seven-year-old and eight- to ten-year-old American children from both fundamentalist Christian communities and nonfundamentalist communities.[14] Evans asked children to rate their agreement with various origin accounts, and she found that regardless of whether parents taught evolution-based origins to their children, children vastly favored creationist accounts of origins for animals and other natural kinds over either evolutionist, artificialist, or emergentist accounts (that animals just appeared). Similarly, psychologist Deborah Kelemen has found that young children have strong inclinations to understand both living and nonliving things as purposeful.[15] They see living and nonliving things as possessing attributes designed to help or to serve themselves or other things. Thus, pointy rocks aren't pointy because some physical process happened to make them pointy; rather, young children tend to accept that rocks are pointy because pointy-ness serves some function, such as keeping them from being sat on. These and other studies have led many psychologists to suspect a bias, arising in childhood, to accept the natural world as created by a nonhuman superbeing. Kelemen has even raised the possibility that children naturally develop as "intuitive theists," and religious instruction merely fills in the forms that already exist in children's minds.[16]

A tendency to see the world as created by a nonhuman superbeing and the ease with which children understand God as the cause of the natural world make acquiring a God concept including supercreative power fairly easy for children. Consequently, a God concept with these powers stands a strong likelihood of successful vertical transmission, ensuring its survival across generations. Further, these early-emerging biases may make a God who has created the world very intuitive and easy to believe in, both in childhood and in adulthood.

Perfect Goodness?

At this point, I lack confidence that a similar argument could be made for the naturalness of perfect moral goodness as a divine trait. However, it should come as no surprise that God, being ascribed all-powerfulness, all-knowingness, and immortality, might also be adored as perfectly good. The superhuman divine properties attributed to God, when present together, might make belief in God's goodness more intuitive than attributing to God fallible morality or even supreme badness.

Indeed, along the same lines that children might overestimate all agents' knowledge, perception, and power, children might overestimate all agents' morality. That is, they assume supermorality until they gain enough evidence to the contrary (such as by observing that others act immorally or being confronted with their own immoral behavior). They then learn the various moral shortcomings of themselves and others but with proper theological encouragement may retain the idea that God is perfectly moral. The idea that God, and perhaps only God, is perfectly good (morally) may turn out to have a fairly strong intuitive, nonreflective foundation based on our nonreflective beliefs regarding the relationship between knowledge and morality and the relationship between desires and actions.

As intuitive moral realists, holding that there is ultimately one normative moral system, believing that an all-knowing God likewise knows about perfect morality follows naturally. If knowing the moral truth of a situation simply requires knowing all there is to know about the behaviors and intentions involved, then an all-knowing God has perfect moral knowledge.

We assume (because of ToM) that the desires of intentional beings motivate their actions. If I want something, I will act in such a way as to get it. But what might this mean for an all-powerful, immortal God? What could such a being lack or want? Unlike humans, for which we know that frustrated desires often lead to treachery, deceit, and violence to satisfy those desires, it seems that an all-powerful God cannot have frustrated desires. Lacking nothing, God would have no intuitively satisfying reason to behave selfishly, immorally. I am not suggesting that a theology could not be developed in which an all-powerful, all-knowing God behaves selfishly and immorally. Rather, such a theology seems to have less intuitive support from the ordinary operation of mental tools. Having no selfish desires makes immoral behaviors for God (if committed) counterintuitive.

Perhaps the only complicating factor is free will. ToM assumes that agents may freely choose how to behave. If God desires people to behave in certain ways, as free beings, people may act in ways that frustrate God's desires. For instance, God could not *make* people *freely* love him. Coerced love isn't love at all. So perhaps in domains that deal with God's interactions with humans, especially humans behaving in ways God might deem objectionable, our intuitive thought might allow for an all-knowing, all-powerful god to act in ways that violate moral norms.

Divine Properties That Are Not Developmentally Privileged

Developmental evidence suggests that children have built-in biases that encourage them to understand and believe (at least in some rudimentary sense) in super-knowing, superperceiving, immortal, superpowerful creator gods. God concepts (such as those in Christianity, Islam, Judaism, and some forms of Hinduism) that have these properties enjoy some transmission advantages over other god concepts. Thus, *once introduced into a population*, God concepts hold strong promise to spread rapidly and gain tenacious adherents. The histories of Christianity and Islam illustrate this claim.

However, not all properties commonly credited to God receive any special support. Indeed, some features of God are downright difficult for kids, let alone adults, to understand. One God existing as three persons, as claimed in Christianity by some formulations, is logically possible but does not spring easily from nonreflective beliefs. The Trinity is a fine example of a belief that is believed only on a reflective level, receiving no nonreflective support. The notion that God is nontemporal or somehow outside of time, a belief of many Christians, Jews, and Muslims, also proves difficult for mental tools to comprehend in any consistent manner. A third example of a God property with no special natural support is omnipresence or having no spatial location. The Divine having nonnatural spatial properties occurs in the Abrahamic religions and many others, including forms of Hinduism. However, the widespread nature of this theological idea does not make it very natural in the sense that being superknowing or immortal is natural. Children and adults may easily think about God as being very large or living in the sky or existing somewhere outside the universe like a person watching a fishbowl, but to conceive of God as having absolutely no location in space or being everywhere in space presents conceptual difficulties. In chapter I, I mentioned the difference between people's explicitly embraced theological concepts and those god concepts used in the real-time production of thoughts, explanations, and predictions. In the narrative comprehension experiments that documented these differences, the properties that were especially hard to maintain when trying to understand and remember the stories were God being nonspatial and nontemporal.

Is God Really Minimally Counterintuitive?

At first glance, God seems far more counterintuitive than would qualify as minimally counterintuitive (MCI; chapter 2). God has funny physical, biological, and psychological properties. So much for one or two violations of intuitive expectations. But a closer look at developmental evidence suggests that many of God's fancier properties are not counterintuitive at all. ToM allows for a mind to be superknowing and superperceiving and to be divorced from a biological body. Likewise, mental tools do not require a disembodied mind to be mortal. We have no reason to believe that God's superpowers present any special difficulty. On the contrary, mental tools suggest that someone has intelligently designed much of the natural world and may willingly embrace God as the Creator. On careful examination, it may be that God's only counterintuitive properties concern God's physicality, such as being omnipresent or having no location in space and time. If so, God nicely fits the parameters for a minimally counterintuitive concept, or MCI.

Additional Factors That Favor the Abrahamic Religions

Add the processes described in the first five chapters of this book to the developmental biases discussed in this chapter, and the monotheisms traced back to Abraham enjoy very special selective advantages over most other religions. Not only does the concept of God enjoy the horizontal transmission advantages due to being MCI, serving as a reasonable target for the activities of HADD and ToM and having the knowledge and power to be easily tied into moral and other social concerns, but God meets a broad range of developmental biases encouraging vertical spread of belief as well. In this section, I amplify a bit further two of the nondevelopmental strengths of the concept of God.

Rituals in the Abrahamic Traditions

In chapter 5, I mentioned that rituals with strong conceptual control stand a greater likelihood of survival than others and, consequently, serve to support rather than undermine the theological foundations from which they spring forth. The ritual systems of Christianity, Islam, and Judaism consist almost entirely of these rituals with strong conceptual control. Many local religions folded (or are folding) under competition from other faiths and from scientific and philosophical inquiry in part because their ritual systems lack the conceptual control to survive changing demands of validity. Shamans, traditional healers, and other spiritual leaders have had to learn about modern medicine to retain their positions of religious leadership, whereas imams, priests, and rabbis have had to make few if any procedural adjustments to ritual performances. They were never in the primary business of bringing rain, healing the sick, making crops grow, making people beautiful, or ensuring the birth of boys. So any failure in these areas or any ability for science and technology to do better at explaining or manipulating these domains has had much less impact on these religions.

Being Generally Superknowing

Gods come in different flavors around the world. Some know a lot about a lot, with the Abrahamic God being a limiting case: knowing everything. Other gods know everything about a particular domain, such as the forest or domestic life. Other gods do not have particularly special minds; they just have been around a long time or can learn things people can't because of their keen eavesdropping abilities that invisibility affords. Still other gods are fairly dumb, easily deceived and requiring information to be deliberately brought to them in just the right way.

Knowing that other beings have limited access to information is essential for social interaction. (One feature of severe autism, a disorder characterized by an inability to have normal social relations, is not being able to calculate the limits of others' knowledge and beliefs.)[17] As mentioned in chapter 4, agents that know something of particular relevance to you, especially related to survival or reproduction, demand greater attention. Such beings possess "strategic information." These agents may be able to impart to us information that is valuable in its own right or that increases our social standing (because someone else might want the information). Thus, gods who have this property are more likely to be pondered and transmitted than gods whose knowledge is trivial or irrelevant. God, who knows everything, certainly has strategic information. In fact, God has *all* the strategic information and is thereby relevant in many different contexts. Unlike the Maya "Masters of the Forest," who know everything about the forest,[18] God knows everything strategic about the forest and the home and wherever else.

By knowing about strategic information in every domain of human concern, God becomes relevant to thought in many different contexts. Whether I am concerned about the weather, the harvest, whether my neighbor is stealing from me, the behavior of my children, or the actions of faraway government officials, God knows and may be concerned and involved. Being potentially involved in so many different spheres broadens the range of mental tools that may form nonreflective belief in God and increases the opportunities to exercise (and thereby strengthen) these nonreflective beliefs. Thus, in comparison with gods who know little or operate only in restricted domains, the concept of God may have more opportunity to be finely enmeshed in a spectrum of activities of thought and action and hence be spread and believed.

Is Monotheism Privileged?

I have argued that a superknowing, superperceiving, superpowerful, immortal, and (perhaps) supergood god possesses strong selective advantages, such that once it is introduced, belief in such a god should spread quite well. This supergod concept matches well (but not perfectly) with the God of Christianity, Islam, and Judaism, and other religious traditions as well. However, belief in a deity such as God does not preclude belief in minor gods, particularly ghosts and ancestor spirits. As discussed in chapter 4, the death of familiar people and the subsequent presence of a corpse and HADD experiences consonant with the deceased continuing to act easily prompt belief in ghosts or ancestor spirits. Nothing in the previous discussion precludes the possibility that these spirits (or others) might act locally while a supreme God takes care of cosmic business or serves in a management capacity. I find the historical fact that ancestor worship, saint cults, and other peripheral religious activities continue to exist alongside "monotheistic" traditions unsurprising. Monotheism does not appear to be a cognitively privileged form of theology except perhaps through considerations of parsimony.

A Progress Report

Belief in God (or gods) comes from the same mental processes that the vast majority of beliefs come from: the operation of mostly nonconscious mental tools. These mental tools give us nonreflective beliefs that we use automatically to make sense of the world around us, to generate inferences, to make predictions, and to explain things "off the cuff" or "on the fly." When reflectively determining what we believe, these nonreflective beliefs serve as our first and best guesses. Unless we have compelling reflectively accessible reasons to believe otherwise, the tabulation of our nonreflective beliefs becomes our reflective beliefs.

The way our minds are put together encourages us to nonreflectively (and hence reflectively) believe in gods generally and God particularly:

- We find MCI agent concepts particularly memorable and attention demanding because of their peculiar fit with intuitive expectations of mental tools plus strong inferential potential.[19]
- Our HADD, working with an aggressive ToM tool, prompts us to find agency among ambiguous information around us. We eagerly search and often find evidence of agents acting around us. Such a tendency warmly receives the idea of gods and makes belief in gods very natural.
- Gods that have special physical properties (such as invisibility) or special mental properties (such as being superperceiving, superknowing, or able to read minds) likewise get easily incorporated into reasoning about social interactions and moral concerns. As agents with "strategic information," we find them important as potential allies or enemies and incorporate them into many different spheres of reasoning, thus enhancing their nonreflective credibility.
- The way two different systems of mental tools deal with the death of people encourages us to believe in life after death and to find reasoning about disembodied minds very natural. Our intuitive assumption that mental processes continue after death may be married with HADD experiences that the dead person has acted and thus encourage belief in ghosts or ancestor spirits.

- Religious actions, including ceremonies, rituals, and prayer, encourage belief in gods. Acting as if gods exist serves to strengthen our resolve that they do. Observing others act as if gods exists serves as testimony that others likewise have reasons to believe in gods. Some particularly emotional religious events even make us *feel* the activity of the divine.
- Concepts of God (as in Christianity, Islam, or Judaism) find special encouragement through the way our mental tools develop. In childhood, our standard, default assumption is that people and God are superknowing, superperceiving, and superpowerful. We must work to learn that this is not so of people, whereas theologically appropriate notions of God come with little struggle. We find the idea that the natural world was designed by a god very natural to accept and contrary notions (such as evolution accounting for life as we know it) peculiar. We find the notions of God being immortal easier to understand and accept than human mortality. Children may find the notion of a supergod being supergood an easy assumption or natural extension of God's other properties.

These observations imply that there is nothing particularly strange about believing in gods. In fact, belief in gods in human groups may be an inevitable consequence of the sorts of minds we are born with in the sort of world we are born into. More specifically, belief in God may be among the most selectively privileged of religious beliefs.

Notes

1. Though these religious traditions may have advantages over others because their central God concepts enjoy additional advantages over those of other religions, this claim does not imply that the adoption of these traditions is inevitable. The case of Hindu India is instructive in this regard. Periods of conquest, colonization, and missionization by Muslims and Christians has not left India predominantly Muslim or Christian. These religious traditions have not largely become acquired. However, Hindus today do commonly embrace superattributes of their major gods, such as Shiva, Vishnu, and Brahma—attributes comparable to the superattributes of the Christian God and the Muslim Allah. Though the Abrahamic religious traditions have not been terribly contagious in India, the supergod concept I argue is quite natural and is common to Abrahamic traditions; indeed, it has become very common in India. I also do not mean to suggest that the relative success of religions can be wholly explained by cognitive factors. Social, political, and other historical factors undoubtedly contribute as well. For example, in China, a supergod concept has remained fairly scarce despite missionary efforts.

2. Rebekah Richert and I have presented this thesis and more detailed summaries of supporting developmental experiments elsewhere (Barrett & Richert, 2003).

3. For a review, see Wellman, Cross, and Watson (2001).

4. Barrett, Richert, and Driesenga (2001).

5. Knight, Sousa, Barrett, and Atran (in press).

6. Barrett, Newman, and Richert (2003). In a similar line of research examining children's understanding of the role of previous knowledge in forming beliefs, the same sort of pattern emerged. Three- through seven-year-old American Christian children were interviewed on three tasks, all of which were concerned with the general question: Do children consider the role of visual access *and* previous knowledge in predicting what their mothers, a dog, and God would know about a display? All three tasks used the same basic form. First, the experimenter presented children with a display that could not be fully understood initially and asked whether the children's mothers, a dog, or God would be able to understand the display. Second, the experimenter provided the relevant information for understanding the display to the children but not to the other agents. Finally, the experimenter asked the children again if their mothers, a dog, or God would be able to understand the display under the same initial conditions.

In one task, the experimenter presented the children with a picture that was covered to the extent that the actual content of the picture was impossible to discern through the visible part. Each child was asked if he or she, his or her mother, a dog, or God would know what the entire drawing depicted. The entire picture was revealed, then partially occluded as before, and then the questions were repeated. In a secret code task, the experimenter showed children three unfamiliar symbols and told them that each stood for something. The experimenter asked whether the child and/or each of the three agents would know what one of the symbols meant. The questions were asked again after each symbol was explained. In a secret game task, the experimenter began playing a novel game. After children said that they did not know what the experimenter was doing, the experimenter asked whether each of the three agents would know what the experimenter was doing. Then the experimenter explained the activity to be a secret game invented by the experimenter and repeated the questions.

7. Another way to interpret what might be going on with children in these tasks is consistent with Piaget's claim that young children are egocentric with regard to determining what others know. Instead of anthropomorphizing, perhaps children simply use a heuristic that amounts to "if I know it, then others know it." Through development, children learn that this is not always the case, though the heuristic remains fruitful in many situations. I do not disagree that such egocentric reasoning could be at play in these studies I have presented. Note, however, that such an account still predicts (accurately) that children will have more difficulty understanding their parents' beliefs accurately compared with understanding God's beliefs. Further, in the tasks employing an understanding of previous knowledge for interpreting visual displays (such as the partially covered picture), children showed a strong tendency to revise their estimates of their mothers' beliefs on the basis of their own knowledge but showed a weaker inclination when reasoning about a dog and no such strategy for estimating God's beliefs regarding the displays. This casts some doubt on the egocentrism hypothesis as applied to nonhuman agents. Perhaps even preschool-aged children possess sensitivity to the fact that other people may be better targets of an analogy or simulation than nonhumans when using their own minds as the analogy's source.

8. Barrett et al. (2001), experiment 3.

9. Richert and Barrett (in press). Another group of American children (ages three to seven) predicted the seeing, hearing, and smelling not only of humans but also of animals with special senses and God. For the visual task, children saw a white piece of paper with a small yellow happy face in the center that was approximately one centimeter across and could be seen only when close to the paper. The hearing task involved a standard tape recorder/player and a tape of various children's songs playing very softly. The smelling task used a 35-mm film container with a small slit cut in the lid and peanut butter inside. Initially, in each condition, children reported they could not perceive the stimulus. Then children were asked to move closely enough to each stimulus to either see, hear, or smell it and to return to their original position. All children first reported their own perception and then predicted the perspectives of a special agent (an eagle with special eyes, a fox with special ears, or a dog with a special nose), a monkey, a human puppet, and God.

10. Gimenez, Guerrero, and Harris (in press). The questions were the following:

1. "Right now there aren't any dinosaurs in the world. But a long time ago there were lots of dinosaurs in the world, like this (show picture). Now what about _____? When there were dinosaurs in the world, did _____ exist?"
2. "Right now you're a little boy/girl but a long time ago you were a little baby right? How about _____? Was s/he a little baby a long time ago?"
3. "What's going to happen to _____ next year and the year after that? Will he get older and older or will he stay just the same?"
4. "What will happen to _____ a long, long time from now? Will _____ die or will s/he go on living for ever and ever?"

11. Piaget (1929).
12. Petrovich (1997).
13. Petrovich (1999).
14. Evans (2001).
15. Kelemen (1999a, 1999b, 1999c, 1999d).
16. Kelemen (in press).
17. Baron-Cohen (1995).
18. See, for instance, Knight et al. (in press).

19. Perhaps by this point it may be clear that what counts as "minimally counterintuitive" includes a fair number of superproperties that seem striking and anything but ordinary. But recall that being bizarre and being counterintuitive are two different things.

The Naturalness of Believing in Minds: **7**
An Analog for Understanding Belief in God

B ELIEF THAT PEOPLE HAVE MINDS is nearly universal. People all around the world believe that others have consciously accessible percepts, beliefs, desires, memories, and thoughts. That is, they believe in minds. Even preschool-aged children believe in minds—with little or no direct tuition on the subject. How often do parents or teachers spell out to four-year-olds that others have beliefs, desires, and so forth? Essentially never. Yet they believe similarly to adults about the mental lives of others. The commonness of the belief in minds testifies to the naturalness of this belief.

The sheer obviousness of others' minds obscures some similarities between believing in God and believing in other minds. I have hinted at these parallels earlier, but in this chapter, I directly present a case that believing in other minds and believing in God are comparably natural beliefs. One is not markedly more strange or bizarre than the other. Believing that other humans have minds arises from many of the same mental tools and environmental information from which belief in gods or God comes.

Some Observations about Belief in Minds

Before turning to specifically how people come to believe in minds, allow me a few observations about belief in minds. First, belief in minds is not empirically supported. Second, belief in minds may occur both nonreflectively and reflectively. Finally, belief in minds is obstinately universal.

First, as with many theological beliefs, believing that other humans have minds is not empirically verifiable. Perhaps surprisingly, no scientific evidence exists that proves people have minds. Indeed, such direct evidence of minds falls beyond the realm of science because minds (as believed in) are experiential and not material.

This claim may seem shocking. After all, isn't psychological science the study of minds? Ultimately, what psychologists study is human behavior, including the behavior of brains and nervous systems. Psychologists and cognitive scientists *interpret* behaviors in terms of mental states and the function of minds. However, *minds* are not accessible to direct investigation and have not even been proven to exist. Similarly, the existence of minds is not falsifiable. That is, they cannot be proven to *not* exist. Minds are invisible, intangible, and immaterial (sound like God?)—not the stuff that science can prove or disprove, even if minds seem like good, reasonable explanations of a huge number of empirically verifiable behaviors. It follows from the observation that minds cannot be empirically verified or falsified that people do not simply believe in minds because they have carefully considered the scientific evidence for and against the existence of minds.

Indeed, belief in minds, like so many broadly held beliefs, does not first arise as a reflective belief. Rather, people typically believe in minds nonreflectively and only sometimes form a reflective belief in minds. Most of our reasoning about others' minds (and our own for that matter) occurs "below the radar," nonconsciously. When my daughter feels sad or frustrated, I naturally wonder what it is that she wants but has been unable to get. Why? It isn't because I consciously recollect that many emotional states are the consequence of the satisfaction or dissatisfaction of desires and my daughter has desires that motivate her actions. I simply *act* as if she has a mind with these properties. This acting *as if* begins very early in life and continues throughout. Very rarely does anyone stop to wonder why we reason about others as we do or if minds really exist.

Naturally, belief in minds—at least in some sense—is essentially universal. Anthropologists traveling to a remote part of the world to observe a never-before-studied group of people will not find that they do not believe in minds. Belief in minds arises from our species' biology working in the sort of environment in which we live. I say belief in minds is *essentially* universal because some small number of academics have suggested and claim to believe that people do not have minds any more than a computer or an earthworm has a mind. But I predict that they do not consistently hold this reflective belief. They do not socially interact in accordance with this belief.

More important, such a peculiar belief about minds (whether or not it is true) simply will not spread. If I told you that the most brilliant scientific minds in the world, after decades of intensive study, have definitively shown that people do not have minds—they do not really think; have beliefs, desires, or emotional states; have experiences; or deliberately do anything—would you believe it? Do you know anyone who would? Such beliefs about minds are so counterintuitive, so much in violation of our natural propensities, that they have no hope of becoming widely held.

That belief in minds typically is nonreflective, is universally and tenaciously held, and does not arise empirically all point to something of an innate reason for why people believe in minds. By innate, I mean that believing in minds is a natural and nearly inevitable consequence of the sort of biology we have, by virtue of being humans and living in the general sort of world in which we live. Believing in minds must come largely from the sorts of minds we have.

Specifically, we believe in others having minds because of the activities of two largely nonconscious mental tools: the hypersensitive agency detection device (HADD) and the Theory of Mind (ToM) tool. By recognizing people as known agents and their "self-propelled" actions, HADD registers people as intentional beings—beings that initiate action on the basis of internal states and not merely mechanistically responding to events in the environment. That is, HADD generates a nonreflective belief that people have some sort of mind. As discussed previously, once HADD identifies something as an agent, it passes on this nonreflective belief to many other mental tools, foremost of which is the ToM tool. ToM attributes beliefs, desires, percepts, and other mental states to agents to try to make sense of their actions and to predict their future actions. To put it another way, once HADD believes people have a mind of sorts, ToM fills in the details about the properties of the mind.

Once HADD and ToM have produced belief in others' minds, numerous other mental tools dealing with social interactions in many different contexts, social roles, social exchange, and so forth happily continue reasoning about people as if they have minds. Thus, a huge number of mental tools (and related experiences) all converge on the nonreflective belief in minds. When asked to reflectively consider whether people have minds, this chorus of mental tools sings out in unison a deafening affirmation. Belief in minds is thoroughly intuitive and nearly impossible to resist.

God and Other Minds

Philosopher Alvin Plantinga once penned a book in which he argued that belief in God is as rationally justifiable as belief in other minds.[1] In brief (and risking oversimplification), belief in the existence of minds does not arise through any empirical or deductive means but is somehow self-evident or foundational. Likewise, he suggests, for many believers in God, the existence of God is similarly foundational. That is, one cannot attack belief in God as unjustified on empirical grounds or failure of logical proofs and hold that belief in minds is justified, as the existence of minds fails on the same grounds.

The strength of Plantinga's argument lies in the assumption that readers do find belief in other minds rationally justified. But for the argument to work, the analogy between believing in other minds and believing in God (and God's mind) must be tight as well. Placing aside both whether God and other minds do in fact exist and how philosophers come to believe in God and other minds, *how* ordinary people come to believe in God and other minds is strikingly similar.

To begin, belief in neither God nor other minds arises from measurable, physical proof. Neither God nor minds are physical objects that can be directly observed. Rather, only the consequences of their activities on the physical, material world serve as evidence for their existence.

Both belief in God and belief in other minds arise from the operations of nonconscious mental tools generating a nonreflective belief. Other minds and God receive affirmation from a huge number of mental tools, experiences, and memories. Of course, foremost among these tools are HADD and ToM.

Perhaps surprisingly, belief in both God and other minds develops throughout a person's childhood in part because of cultural inputs—from communicated ideas about God and other minds. When a child is forming ideas about others' minds, parents and others tell them about people's beliefs, desires, feelings, percepts, and so forth. A parent's simple statement such as, "I can't see you so I don't know where you are," cryptically communicates that the parent can *see* things (a mental activity) and *know* things (another mental activity) and that knowing is somehow connected to seeing. Such causal utterances help develop how we come to believe in other minds.

Similarly, theists do not typically say to their kids, "God is this being with a super mind that has beliefs, desires, and percepts." Rather, they say things like, "I guess God wanted that to happen," or, "God knows that you are upset." Most of children's education about God's mind (and other features) and of other minds consists of these fragmentary, indirect suggestions interpreted and filled in by mental tools—tools biased to attribute minds with all their standard properties given only a little push.

Just as the particulars of how people talk about God (or gods) in children's environments influence the particular concept of God (or gods) a child acquires, how people talk about minds may influence the specific understanding of mind that becomes embraced. If I grow up hearing that elderly people are wise but forgetful and that teenagers are emotional and volatile, I may come to characterize these different classes of minds differently and have different expectations about their behaviors. Likewise, if I grow up hearing that the ancestors know when you think bad things about them but the forest spirits can be tricked by using cryptic speech about your intentions, I may form very different ideas of the minds of these different gods.

Once these nonreflective beliefs in minds arise through the activity of HADD and ToM, numerous other mental tools operate on these beliefs and thereby encourage and fortify reflective belief in God and other minds. I described many of the higher-level operations involving god concepts in previous chapters. Comparable activities play on the identification of people as agents. For instance, in social exchange with others, we assume (and thus reinforce) the idea that the parties in exchange relationships have minds. We expect commensurate giving because the other *knows* that such giving is right. We can delay exchanges over time because we assume that others *remember* our gifts. We assume that fair exchanges make others *feel* satisfied. In this way, our mental tools, especially concerned with social exchange, harmoniously coexist and mutually reinforce belief in minds.

Some Possible Weaknesses of the Analogy

Despite the numerous parallels in how belief in God (or gods) and belief in other minds arise, some differences exist as well. These differences do account for the more uniform belief in other minds as compared with gods but do not weaken the claim that belief in gods is a natural and quite expected part of being human. (Nor do these differences between how god concepts become embraced and how we come to believe in minds weaken Plantinga's argument. His argument is sustained by epistemological concerns that remain quite independent of *how* we come to believe. Rather, they concern whether we *should* believe.)

People Have Bodies

Though we cannot directly observe others' minds to support belief in them, doesn't the fact that others have bodies encourage belief that other humans have minds? And doesn't belief in God lack this prompt? Sure. But the connection between minds and bodies is not simple or solid. We do not come to think that other people have minds because they have bodies. Rather, we first detect agentive action acting on or through human bodies and then attribute minds.

Belief in God is particularly similar to the human ability to reason about nonpresent (people's) minds, hypothetical persons, and minds that might account for noticed traces and artifacts. From very early in life, babies learn to appreciate that people do not fail to exist just because their bodies aren't perceivable. Imagine if detecting a body were required for believing in a mind. Activities we take for granted, such as talking with a stranger on the phone, sending a message through the mail, or even talking to someone in the next room, would be strange, disorienting events.

That believing in and reasoning about minds remains divorced from bodies becomes particularly clear in considering mind–body dualism. Until recently, in historical terms, even philosophers regarded minds as separate from bodies. Descartes championed such a view of the mind. Further, we can easily imagine minds being switched between two different individuals—indeed, movies and stories sometimes play on such premises—with little or no concern for how the mind may be shaped by the body it is in. In teaching introductory psychology, one of the more difficult concepts to impress on students is the embodied nature of the human mind. Such a concept is hard to teach because it is counterintuitive. Our nonreflective mental tools don't intuitively see minds as linked to bodies.

This divide between minds and bodies helps explain the ease with which we can imagine (and even believe) that animals of nearly any level of physiological complexity have minds—perhaps dumb minds, but minds nonetheless. People easily, perhaps automatically, believe that dogs, cats, birds, and even goldfish have beliefs, desires, percepts, and experiences and enjoy willfully initiated behavior. To her parents' chagrin, as a toddler my daughter would even treat earthworms as volitional beings with minds, talking to them, scolding them, coddling them, and reading them stories. Somehow her HADD and ToM found legitimate targets in even these primitive forms.

I should note that not all god concepts lack bodies or physicality. To this point, I have been discussing the more familiar sort of god who is immaterial. But various gods possess bodies or physical forms. Gods sometimes take the form of mountains (especially volcanic ones). Some gods amount to thinking, listening, acting trees. Some gods inhabit animal forms. Many gods have been identified in human or humanlike bodies. Jesus Christ is one obvious example. Hindus typically describe their gods, such as Shiva, Vishnu, Krishna, Rama, and others, as embodied in humanlike forms. For these cases of gods, the differences between belief in human minds and belief in the gods becomes even slighter.

What about Human Brains?

For a special version of the objection that having a human body promotes believing in others' minds, consider the role of the brain. We know that brains house minds and that human bodies house brains. Doesn't that give belief in others' minds a big edge over belief in gods? Such an argument ignores the fact that, historically, the role of the brain as a substrate for the mind has only been known recently. For ages, people have assumed that others have minds without knowing anything about brains. Likewise, children believe in minds without the benefit of brain knowledge.

Minds over Matter

One potential objection to the analogy concerns God's ability to manipulate or act on the physical world without being a physical, embodied being. Isn't God's agency—a nonmaterial acting on a material—importantly different from human agency—a physical being acting physically? Perhaps surprisingly, no. Actually, we intuitively recognize our own agency and that of other people's as being cases of mind over matter. I desire for a physical object to move, for instance, and it does. Of course, I refer to moving my own body. A corollary of mind–body dualism is that the nonphysical mind operates on the material body all the time. This relationship strikes us as wholly intuitive.[2] Thus, in principle, a god acting directly on the material world presents no special difficulties.

Other Minds Are Human

One way in which we do more easily believe in other people's minds than believe in God is that people have human form. From birth, people have a special sensitivity to finding human faces in the environment, and before long, humanlike forms may trigger HADD. Agentive action repeatedly pairs with human form as humans behave in ways that HADD believes suggests agency. This close link between having a human form and being a mental agent becomes impressively strong over time, but never does human form and agency become equated by mental tools. A perfectly realistic mannequin may momentarily make us believe it is a person with a mind, but such a belief is readily abandoned without agentlike activity. On the other hand, a disguised, camouflaged, or otherwise unseen person may be detected and treated as a mental being if it exhibits purposeful action. This ability to find agents that do not remotely resemble humans (or even have bodies) suggests that the advantage other minds have over God by virtue of possessing a human form is minimal.

Introspective Advantages of Having a Human Mind

The fact that we ourselves have human minds may assist us in discovering them in other humans. The quasi-Cartesian dictum "I think, therefore I am" may be recast as "I think, therefore I have a mind." Our introspective experiences of our own minds give us additional nonreflective (and hence reflective) reason to believe in our own minds. As other humans' physical forms, expressions, and activities resemble our own, we may have strong impetus to suppose that others have minds like ours.

One school of thought in the study of ToM emphasizes the role of *simulation* in reasoning about other minds.[3] To understand the mental states of others, we put ourselves in others' shoes, so to speak. We ask, "If I were she, what would I see, hear, think, feel, or want?" Through simulating what it would be like to be others, we form good guesses about their mental states. We find simulation easiest and more complete when we can easily map our own mental states onto the other. Thus, the more similarities, including physical and behavioral ones, that we share with the target, the easier it is for us to simulate the other's mental states. I find imagining what my brother might be thinking much easier than imagining the mental life of a goldfish.

Simulation theory represents a common but controversial position in the theory-of-mind field. Among other concerns, critics point to the surprisingly poor access that people (especially children) have to their own mental states. Sometimes we don't know what has upset us. Sometimes we don't know what emotion we are experiencing. Often we only have faint, nonreflective knowledge of our own beliefs. Often we don't know our own minds. Critics, then, argue that our ability to reason about others' minds does not take the form of a series of simulations but rather is a set of "theories" or rule-like propositions. If we see an unhappy child, instead of trying to put ourselves in the child's place and simulating her mind, we simply reason, "People get unhappy when they don't get what they want. Therefore, the girl must have an unsatisfied desire." Such reasoning about minds is awkwardly but memorably referred to as "theory theory" in contrast to "simulation theory."[4]

My own research in the theory-of-mind area has led me to believe that the truth lies between the two positions (as often seems the case). We conduct simulations to generate ideas about someone else's mental states. Using these simulations, we also form "theories" about minds that eliminate the need for redundant simulations. If I see someone greedily stuffing food in his mouth, I just know via theories of mind that he is hungry and likes this food. I also predict he will be in a good, satisfied mood and sated before long. I need not simulate any of this. But when my theories fail, as when someone behaves inexplicably, I simulate. I may wonder what I would be thinking or feeling if I were in her shoes. Hence, the ability to simulate may be most important when reasoning about the minds of unfamiliar agents—agents whom we know less about or who are not predictable in their activities. Our ability to simulate mental states might be most important in reasoning about beings such as gods only until we become facile in such theological thought.

Note, however, that whether or not simulation (or theory-of-mind formation) favors the understanding of human minds over God's mind, attribution of a mind has already taken place before such functions operate. Belief in God or others' minds may be only secondarily impacted by how we then reason about those minds.

The Case of Animal Minds

Of course, other people aren't the only ones we believe have minds. I have stressed the comparison between belief in God (or gods) and the belief in human minds because of the noncontroversial nature of the belief in human minds. More controversially, people commonly believe that animals have minds—perhaps not very intelligent minds but minds nonetheless.

We see dogs as *wanting* to play, *feeling* happy, and trying to *figure* out how to get food out of bags. Cats *believe* that a spot of light is a small animal, *enjoy* playing with mice, and *decide* not to come when called. We even attribute mental states and willful behavior to animals such as fish. Anglers try to trick fish into *believing* bits of plastic and metal are desired prey. Fish *feel* scared, get *suspicious*, and *choose* not to bite.

Most of these beliefs about animal minds, though arising nonreflectively, commonly reach reflective status without being seen as irrational, foolish, or naive. As in believing in human minds, belief in animal minds arises from the activity of HADD and ToM. Purposeful and self-propelled action triggers HADD to recognize these animals as agents with minds. ToM automatically fills in the details. In the absence of sufficient, consciously accessible reasons to believe otherwise, these nonreflective beliefs become accepted reflectively. That animals have minds feels intuitive.

To a greater degree than with human minds, scientists studying animal behavior and physiology have cast doubt on the intuitive notion that animals (especially relatively simple ones) have minds. They argue that more and more of animal behavior may be understood as almost mechanistic reactions to particular stimuli—sometimes accumulated exposure to stimuli over time. A cat does not "think" that a spot of light from a flashlight is a mouse or any other animal. Rather, the light spot triggers a series of biochemical reactions in the cat's nervous system, prompting it to move its body in a way we identify as predatory. The cat does not *think* or *believe* anything. They have no minds. They behave on the basis of a series of complex "instincts" or "reflexes" similar to how flowers open their petals to the sun and just as nonmental.

Now, I imagine for most readers—even for those who don't care for cats—would find this scientific description of cats' behavior fairly sterile and *intuitively* unsatisfying. Consequently, we find the idea that cats (as well as dogs, cows, parrots, dolphins, and so on) do *not* have minds implausible. It receives no intuitive support because it contradicts nonreflective beliefs.

The Incredibleness of Not Believing in Minds

Imagine a university professor from an elite institution—maybe a scientist—telling you that believing that people have minds is irrational. After all, we have no scientific evidence that minds exist, and more and more behavior that we have traditionally explained by referring to minds can now be explained through other, scientific means. Consequently, the professor might argue, belief in minds is unwarranted. Convinced? Me neither.

Unsurprisingly, though some scientists occasionally make such arguments,[5] disbelief in human (or animal) minds has not caught on even among highly educated people, let alone in the general populace of the world. The idea that we do not have minds strikes us as too counterintuitive to be credible. As with many reflective beliefs with weak nonreflective foundations, even within the scientific circles in which minds are doubted, such a position does not consistently motivate behavior. These scientists may deny that people really have beliefs but then talk about others' beliefs and seek to change them through conventional, mentalistic means. They may deny that people willfully do anything but still hold their children responsible for "willful" disobedience. They may deny desires but still seek to satisfy the desires of their spouses. This inability to wholly believe that minds do not exist does not mean that minds definitely do exist. Simply, belief in minds is perfectly understandable and does not merit ridicule. Belief in minds is *natural*. Yet belief in God receives unjust condemnation.

The Incredibleness of Not Believing in God

Academics, as well as other folk with generous formal education (primarily social scientists), often ridicule religious beliefs, particularly belief in God, on the same grounds that should disqualify belief in minds as "irrational." Belief in God cannot be scientifically proven (or disproven); neither can belief in other minds. Science (including psychological and cognitive sciences) offers explanations for phenomena previously attributed to God much as mental phenomena are alternatively explained by psychological scientists.

The tenacity with which religious believers adhere to their belief in God astounds many nonbelievers, particularly in the academy. "Why *would* anyone believe in God?" Congruent with the description given in previous chapters, the answer to this question mirrors another: "Why would anyone believe in others' minds?" People believe because such belief is intuitively satisfying. It matches nonreflective beliefs generated by a host of mental tools converging on the same thing: minds and gods are out there.

That belief in God (or gods) but not minds is discounted out of hand as absurd betrays a lack of intellectual honesty. Much as disagreements over the minds of animals hinge on political and practical considerations regarding the use and treatment of animals, typically, "scientistic" attacks on belief in God arise more from political and practical motivations, prejudice, and ethnocentrism than from a fair appraisal of the legitimacy of belief. These same scientists who reflexively assert that belief in *any and all* gods is unwarranted on scientific grounds blindly ignore the countless other beliefs they hold near and dear that find themselves in the same scientific predicament as God. For example, we cannot *scientifically* prove that time flows steadily, that the past has actually existed, that the laws of physics will hold in the future, that our own mind can be trusted, or that others even exist. On the top of this list of unproven assertions is belief in minds.

Notes

1. Plantinga (1990).

2. I thank Pascal Boyer for this observation.

3. For example, Goldman (1992); Gordon (1986, 1992); Harris (1992).

4. For a discussion of these various theoretical issues from a variety of perspectives, see Carruthers and Smith (1996).

5. I have heard such claims made in discussion on numerous occasions, but it is still fairly rare to make such arguments in print.

Why Would Anyone *Not* Believe in God? 8

TO THIS POINT, I have tried to answer the question "Why would anyone believe in God?" I contend that people commonly believe in gods because of
the way our minds work in the sorts of natural and social environments
we inhabit.

We believe most of what we do—including what we believe exists in the
world—because of the operation of numerous mental tools, operating mostly below conscious awareness. These mental tools, designed to enable rapid processing of
information in various particular domains, generate nonreflective beliefs. When creating what might be called reflective beliefs, unless given strong reason to the contrary, we simply adopt these nonreflective beliefs as reflective beliefs. Consequently,
any belief, such as a belief in God, that receives strong support from mental tools,
that is nonreflectively believed, is a strong candidate for widespread reflective belief.

Our minds find ideas about minimally counterintuitive (MCI) agents particularly memorable and easy to share with others. These MCI agents also prove very
useful in making sense of or addressing numerous phenomena around us. Additionally, a particular mental tool, the hypersensitive agency detection device
(HADD) easily detects agents and agency in the environment given incomplete or
inconclusive evidence. Though the bulk of these agent detections may be rejected
after further evidence gathering, some become recognized as gods. If the detected
agent or agency is attributed to a known god, such HADD activity encourages belief in and the spread of the god concept. In rare cases, HADD could also encourage the postulation of a new god.

Further, because gods are agents with special properties, such as having super-
access to "strategic information" governing human affairs, they also receive support from a host of mental tools related to human interaction. When reasoning

morally, incorporating the presence of a god into consideration mutually reinforces our intuitions that moral rules exist objectively. Thus, the notion that a god sees someone's immoral behavior and disapproves is quite intuitive. Because moral reasoning impacts social exchange, status, and other relations, it is easy for belief in a god or gods to become intricately connected to the actions of numerous other mental tools.

Concepts of a superpowerful, superperceiving, superknowing, and immortal supreme God receive further support and encouragement by the character of natural human conceptual development. Children seem to naturally assume that agents have these divine properties and have to learn that people and animals do not have them. Consequently, it is easy for children to learn about God and form a rudimentary, theological notion of God. In this way, God concepts (in comparison with god concepts) may find an even easier time being spread from one generation to the next.

Thus, believing in God is a natural, almost inevitable consequence of the types of minds we have living in the sort of world we inhabit, similar to why it is that people almost universally believe in minds of humans and many animals. We have no scientific or even directly observable evidence for God or minds, yet belief in both is extremely common and tenaciously held. Why? Because both arise from natural workings of the human mind.

But a complete scientific account of belief in God must explain not only why it is that people believe but also why sometimes they don't believe in God or gods. After presenting this argument to colleagues in the academy, I sometimes get these sorts of questions: Well, if religion comes so naturally, what accounts for atheism? Are you saying that atheism is unnatural? But how could it be if so many of us are atheists? In this chapter, I argue that atheism (the disbelief in any gods) as a shared worldview arises only under special conditions and is indeed the exception to the rule. Compared to theism, atheism is relatively unnatural and, unsurprisingly, a very uncommon worldview.

The Difficulty with Being an Atheist

Being an atheist is not easy. In many ways, it just goes against the grain. As odd as it sounds, it isn't natural to reject all supernatural agents. I'm not saying all atheists have the conscious experience of angst over being an atheist or struggle with such a worldview. Much as skilled pianists don't find playing the piano difficult, trained social scientists don't find it particularly difficult to reason statistically, and philosophers don't find it terribly difficult to avoid basic errors of logic, many atheists do not find atheism consciously taxing. In addition to the special environments they thrive in, to which I'll turn shortly, they have become accustomed to or well practiced at such thought. What such fluency masks is the relative difficulty in being an atheist (at least in many environments).

Each of the factors that encourage theism poses challenges to atheism that must be overcome. I'll present four of these factors that pose special problems for atheism and then offer suggestions for how atheists may attempt to solve these problems.

HADD and ToM

As discussed in chapter 3, our mental tools, specifically HADD working with the Theory of Mind (ToM) tool, make us prone to find agents, agency, and the consequences of agency in our environment. Such detections may be satisfied by any number of agent identifications, but the unusual character of them discourages us from positing that the agency is human. Often ghosts, spirits, or gods, fit the job description better. But for the strict atheist, only two options remain: any detected agency could be attributed to natural agents such as humans or animals, or the agency could be rejected. An atheist could reflectively override HADD's detection of agency.

To return to Doug, the farmworker who survived the silo explosion, most theist and atheists alike intuitively detect agency in his story. Our HADDs ask, "*Who* saved him from the silo?" The theist may answer the question with God or angels or with any number of other options, depending on their religious background, and such an answer holds great intuitive satisfaction. The atheist may answer HADD with, "Some unseen coworker saved him." But then ToM asks why Doug didn't see the coworker. The mental tools that store properties of humans would then ask how the coworker managed to lift Doug out of a second-story window. The cacophony of questions from mental tools makes the "human" identification extremely unsatisfying. But the atheist has another option, rejecting the detection of agency: HADD was wrong, and no agent or agency was present. Some unknown physical property protected Doug from the initial explosion and propelled Doug out of the second-floor window unharmed, or it happened just by chance. But this type of explanation is no explanation at all. What it amounts to is a promissory note: I don't know how to explain it, but I'm sure there is an explanation that has nothing to do with agency.

Satisfying HADD's detection of agency with a human (or animal) agent identification often presents difficulty. We know a lot about the properties of people and animals and what they can and cannot do. Just the fact that people and animals are visible makes unseen agency difficult to attribute to them. Our knowledge of people and animals drastically restricts the range of cases for which they may serve as suitable candidates to satisfy HADD.

Rejecting HADD's detection of agency may sound easy, but it is not. One of the strengths of the human mind is its ferocious desire to explain, make sense, and find meaning. If we tell HADD that it has misexplained something, it demands that we come up with a satisfactory counterexplanation. Finding such a counterexplanation is not always simple: it requires conscious, reflective thought; it is slow; and it may require tapping our long-term memories for knowledge we incompletely hold. Even if this cumbersome reasoning process yields a counterexplanation that seems satisfying to the self, others, not sharing the same knowledge base, may find it dissatisfying because of its poor foundation in nonreflective belief systems.

Recall that HADD's insistence that it has detected agency may increase under conditions of urgency, as when survival or physical well-being is on the line. Similarly, denying HADD and settling on a satisfactory counterexplanation in urgent situations may be all the more difficult.

Stories like Doug's are relatively uncommon. Not all instances of HADD experiences present great difficulties to atheists, and the more clever and creative you are, the more likely you are to hit on some counterexplanation that has a ring of plausibility to yourself and others. But HADD experiences are common, occasionally occur when rapid explanation is required, and often cannot be easily explained in purely naturalistic terms.

Moral Realism

Theists may casually go about making moral judgments, feeling guilt for having done something wrong, or feeling moral indignation for having been wronged. A god has seen and agrees with their moral assessment and may reward the just or smite the wicked. If some fortune or misfortune befalls a person, the god may be acting, or the event is a natural consequence of previous actions.

For atheists, things are not so simple. Their intuitive sense of morality continues to function very much like the theists but with no reason for moral certitude. Consequently, atheists, unlike theists, have a burden to concoct theories of morality that justify their moral certainty or abandon it. And abandoning is no easy business, and rarely, if ever, is it done successfully. I may be a champion of moral relativism, regarding morality as completely subjective, right up until I am wronged.

Dealing with Death

Theists may understand that strange sense that a recently departed loved one still cares about them and is aware of things as a simple by-product of the dead still being present in spirit or disembodied form. Visiting the grave and talking to the deceased makes a certain amount of sense. Though the dead typically do not respond, they may understand the affections of the living. For atheists, these feelings and behaviors require other explanation. Denying disembodied agency, atheists have reason to view a dead body, even of a loved one, only as perhaps a reminder of mortality but having the agency and sacredness of a rock on the road. Musing about what a loved one who has died must be thinking or feeling or attempting communication with the dead is utter absurdity. Feel angry at being left behind? Nonsense. Feel betrayed or lonely at another's passing? Rubbish. Such impulses must be regarded only as irrational. Yet there they are.

Overcoming Native Creationism

As suggested in chapter 3 and developed in chapter 6, we may develop as children with a formidable bias toward seeing the natural world as being purposefully designed. Accordingly, children seem eager to embrace creationist accounts of the origins of living things. For atheism to thrive and spread, not only must this bias be overcome by adult atheists, but somehow they must be able to pass their atheism on to their kids, against the objections of their mental tools that tell them the world was created with purposeful design.

Reflective Problems for Atheists

In addition to reinterpreting nonreflective beliefs that suggest superhuman agency, atheism requires combating conscious, reflective arguments for theistic thought. In some ways, the burden for certainty is greater for atheists than for theists. As I have tried to show, the bulk of theists need not reflectively work out reasons for believing in God (or gods). Given the sort of experiences they have, including the suggestion from others that God does exist, belief enjoys such rich intuitive support that no justification seems necessary. (Perhaps this is why some believers are such easy marks for those college professors that are hell-bent on dissuading them of their faith. They have few if any explicit reasons they can articulate for belief.) Atheism, on the other hand, has less in terms of intuitive support but brings more explicit rationale to the table. As a more reflective belief system, frequently intellectually discovered, atheism has more reflective opportunity for being challenged (as well as encouraged). Hence, explicit reasons for theism generally require some attention from the atheist.

Historically, theists have offered various arguments or "proofs" for some sort of god. For instance, teleological cases or arguments appealing to the apparent design and purposefulness of the world historically have held great sway.[1] Nonreflectively, our mental tools for detecting traces of agency and purposeful activity and utility find evidence for design all around. Reflectively, the design of the world seems intuitively reasonable and an easy belief to hold. How, then, is there design? God seems like a reasonable candidate. It wasn't until Darwinism became widely embraced that atheists had a satisfying defense against their own intuitive sense that the world was designed and the congruent claims of theists. Darwinism seemed to offer a god-free explanation for observed order. Though the Darwinist defense actually addresses only order in complex living systems and not the origin of life or the mechanical fine-tuning that many astronomers and physicists have recently noted,[2] such intellectual arguments help bolster the credibility and distribution of atheist beliefs.

Atheists may also have epistemological difficulties that theists (depending on theology) do not have. Theists may confidently hold reflective beliefs operating under the assumption that their mind was designed by an intelligent being to provide truth, at least in many domains. For the atheist, another explanation for the certitude of beliefs must be found, or certitude must be abandoned. If our very existence is a cosmological accident and our minds have been shaped by a series of random mutations whittled by survival pressures (not necessarily demanding truth, only survival and reproduction, as a rat, fly, or bacteria can pull off with their "minds"), then why should we feel confident in any belief? And if we can't feel confident in our beliefs, why do we go through life pretending we can? These questions may have satisfactory answers. The point is that unlike the theist, the atheist has far more explaining to do. This, too, makes atheism harder.

Fighting Back Theism

By listing these examples of problems atheists must face, I do not mean to suggest that theism cannot be successfully challenged and fought back in the lives of large numbers of people. Atheism just requires some special conditions to help it struggle against theism. In the following sections, I list a number of strategies for fighting theistic tendencies.

Strategy 1: Consider Additional Candidates for Belief

As we form beliefs reflectively though "reading off" beliefs from mental tools, the natural tendency toward theistic beliefs must be countered by salient alternative candidates. Since these candidates will not typically come through nonreflective channels, they must be sought explicitly. Someone hoping to be a successful atheist would do well to spend time with other atheists who can help provide naturalistic explanations for events and phenomena that invite theistic thought.

To illustrate, overcoming the natural tendency to see the world as intelligently designed by a god may best be combated by explicitly offering the mental tools a different candidate explanation. When I was a graduate student, a professor at my university prided himself on turning Christians into atheists through the term of his course on evolution. (Never mind that belief in evolution peacefully coexists with Christian theism in many minds.) The reason this course was successful in turning students away from God was because it offered alternative frames for reflectively interpreting mental tool outputs concerning apparent design and purpose in the world. The agency of God was systematically replaced by the agency of natural selection. And I do mean *agency*. One of the embarrassing realities for evolutionary theorists is the difficulty of consistently thinking or talking about natural selection without using mental-states language. At an implicit level, natural selection amounts to a sanitized and scientifically sanctioned "god" that may displace God.

Strategy 2: Reduce Theism-Consistent Outputs from Mental Tools

Since reflective plausibility of God gains strength from the number of mental tools offering confident nonreflective beliefs consonant with God's existence, atheism becomes easier to hold if these nonreflective beliefs can be reduced. But how might this be accomplished since these nonreflective beliefs spring forth from the kinds of minds we have? The answer is to change the environment in which mental tools operate.

STRATEGY 2A: LIMIT HADD OUTPUTS BY REDUCING URGENCY A good specific strategy is to strike at the heart of the primary systems responsible for encouraging nonreflective theistic beliefs: HADD. Recall that HADD becomes especially prone to detect agency (and thereby support theism) in urgent situations. Thus, reduce urgency. It is said that there are no atheists in foxholes, but it is also much harder to be an atheist when your day-to-day activities directly impact the survival of you and your family. If your livelihood is based on subsistence hunting or on agriculture and the decisions you make regularly directly impact how much food you and your family might have, atheism becomes more difficult. Similarly, poverty does not improve the likelihood of becoming an atheist. A wealthier existence typically has less urgency in the specific sense relevant to HADD.

STRATEGY 2B: MAKE SURE HADD SEES ONLY HUMAN AGENCY Of course, HADD and its friend ToM become most problematic for atheism when the agency with which they reason does not appear to be human. Thus, another strategy for fighting theism is to submerge oneself in a context in which the agency all around is obviously human. Little or no room is left to detect ambiguous agency that might be labeled godly. Living in a fully urban setting is a good step in the right direction. Life surrounded by wilderness or natural systems would be a mistake.

Strategy 3: Reduce Secondhand Accounts That Might Become Evidence for God

In chapter 1, I discussed how reflective plausibility of religious beliefs also gains support because existing nonreflective religious beliefs shape and filter memories for experience. This shaping and filtering also applies to the accounts of others' experiences in a religious community. These accounts thus provide supporting evidence for some religious beliefs. Avoiding religious people altogether so that you do not hear their stories would help avoid troublesome "evidence" that seems to support God.

Short of completely avoiding religious people, another strategy is available: become immersed in a pluralistic society in which others' experiences hold little importance to you. In contexts in which everyone is a farmer, everyone is a hunter or gatherer, or everyone's livelihood depends on the annual salmon runs, experiences have common relevance and are hard to ignore. Let's return to Scott Atran's account of the Maya hunter bitten by a deadly viper. For another Maya hunter, this story has tremendous relevance for forest behavior and reinforces existing beliefs about the existence and powers of the forest spirits. But I imagine that most American or European urbanites or suburbanites can easily dismiss the story as a bit puzzling but not worth much careful evaluation. Why not? My hunch is that part of the answer lies not with some inherent incredibility about the event but because the experience of some hunter in Central America has little inherent importance for European or American professionals. We live in a social environment in which there is a great plurality of daily demands and experiences, and consequently others' experiences are (intuitively) a less important database for evaluating beliefs.

Strategy 4: Surround Yourself with Ample Opportunities for Exercising Reflective Thought

As it is nonreflective beliefs that may promote belief in God or gods, plentiful opportunities for overriding nonreflective beliefs may serve as defense against theism. Of course, reflective thought requires time and is helped by a community of others who likewise engage in intellectual exercises. Such an environment provides the luxury of disinterested reflection on issues such as whether gods exist without such musings interfering with successful hunting or harvesting. As I mentioned previously, reflective thought may present problems for atheists for which nonreflective theists need not concern themselves. But if the reflective environment is sufficiently pluralistic and sufficiently nontheistic in orientation, it may still heartily contribute to the successful embrace and spread of atheism.

In these reflective environments, events and phenomena that might encourage theism may be handled with cool consideration, and alternative frames of reasoning may be developed. For example, alleged "miracles" or acts of God may be relabeled as simple chance occurrences, for although "chance" does not qualify as a satisfactory nonreflective explanation, with proper statistical and probabilistic training, "chance" can go a long way toward avoiding needless hypothesizing about why something happened in the reflective mode. Similarly, medical "miracles" or what might be seen as the healing power of a god could be reexplained in the terms of medical science. Those events that may be truly explained could be reflectively explained with no appeal to deities. Those that cannot truly be explained might be labeled in appropriate jargon suggesting that they need not be explained, as in cases of spontaneous remission or placebo effects.

Why Atheism Is Where We See It

Compared with the near inevitability of theism, atheism appears to lack the natural, intuitive support to become a widespread type of worldview. Nevertheless, the past fifty years has seen atheism become fairly widespread in segments of Europe and North America. Though still a minority position—even in some former Soviet-controlled nations where theism was illegal and even in academic communities—atheism seems to have found some fertile soil in the so-called Western world. But why so?

One opinion, popular among atheists, is that theism can exist only with ignorance. Educated people who understand reason and science inevitably reject theism, hence the relative recent rise in atheism among scientifically and technologically advanced societies and its prominence in nations with strong education systems. Whereas this hypothesis strokes elitist egos, it fails to account for the high rate of theism in a well-educated nation such as the United States and for the weak correlation between atheism and education within Europe, Canada, and the United States.[3] Neither does it explain why so many reputable scholars— including philosophers and scientists—are theists. Formal education does impact the success of atheism, but the relationship is not the simple "only dumb people believe in God" that seems so common among academics.

Another opinion, gleaned from Marx and Freud, is that religion amounts to a crutch for the poor, suffering, and disenfranchised of the world. Not surprisingly, then, we find that in communities where technology has reduced mortality, poverty, and suffering, religious belief has also declined. Such a simplistic explanation gains strength on the ability for religious commitment to comfort and to encourage psychological adjustment, which has been well documented by psychologists of religion. However, this account ignores the fact that religion also has the ability to terrorize and oppress. The promise of heaven may make death less threatening, but what about hell? Morality, poverty, and suffering may be related to religious commitment but with more nuance than the "religion as a crutch" hypothesis suggests.

Historically, a small number of individual thinkers in many different societies have rejected belief in gods. However, the markers of the societies in which atheism seems to be able to spread and develop a noticeable following seem to have emerged late in history. Before the industrial revolution, atheism almost did not exist. People might have rejected organized religions, but they did not cease to believe in God or gods of some sort, including ghosts and spirits. The industrial revolution opened the door, but few walked through until after World War II. The distinctive characteristics of societies in which atheism seems to have a foothold include urbanization, industrial or postindustrial economies, enough wealth to support systems of higher education and leisure time, and prominent development of science and technology.

Urban settings contribute to atheism in at least two ways. First, urbanization brings a diversity of people and perspectives into close contact. This diversity of concerns and beliefs may reduce religious thought by providing alternative frames for reflectively interpreting nonreflective beliefs consistent with theism. Similarly, differences in jobs, experiences, and values reduce the intuitive relevance of others' experiences. So what if someone from across town experienced something that seems to support the existence of God? What is that to my life? Second, urbanization reduces the amount of the day-to-day world that has not been designed by humans or is not under the control of humans. As an urban dweller makes sense of the world around, HADD detects agency everywhere. But almost everything is easily and satisfactorily labeled as the consequence of human agency. No need for gods. Even cases of unusual fortune and misfortune may be attributed to anthropomorphic abstractions, such as "society," "the education system," "the market," and "the government."

The distance that urbanization provides from natural systems grows even greater in societies that have primarily industrial or postindustrial economies. City dwellers before the industrial revolution still had a tangible relationship with the seasonal cycles, weather patterns, plagues, blights, and other natural factors that impacted such basic needs as food. Now in the so-called postindustrial era, many living in Canada, Europe, and the United States really have no sense of where food comes from. It seems to grow on the market shelves. If it isn't there, it is because of human mistakes, not because of a storm, drought, or pestilence. The ability to attribute all agency to human agency is enhanced under these economic conditions. Further, the urgency with which HADD searches for agency is reduced. Life and death do not rise and fall on the coming of rain clouds or a successful hunt. The postindustrial urban center regularizes and reduces apparent threats to welfare. Those that remain, such as criminal violence, clearly have human and not divine origins.

We've all heard the saying that there are no atheists in foxholes. A safer claim is that there are no atheists in the preindustrialized world. Subsistence hunter–gatherers, farmers, and others with traditional, organic lifestyles are almost uniformly theists of one sort or another and always have been. With any distribution beyond a few peculiar individuals, true atheism (the rejection of all superhuman agents, including gods, ghosts, ancestors, demons, and spirits) has occurred only in communities largely divorced from natural subsistence and hence only in industrialized or postindustrialized contexts. On examination, the preindustrialized world and foxholes have much in common to encourage theism: survival-related urgency to make sense of the world, a reliance on natural and not human processes for survival, and being surrounded by apparent agency that cannot be simply attributed to human endeavor or simply ignored.

Industrial and postindustrial urban populations enjoy time and resources that provide for the exchange of ideas and for reflection. As labor demands have gone beyond the general knowledge of hunting or farming or even low-skill industrial work, educational systems have developed. The diversity of knowledge required for the diversity of jobs in postindustrial society requires more specialized (that is, less natural) education than in previous societies. Thus, more economic resources have been dedicated to exchanging ideas and opportunities to exercise reflective thought. As I suggested previously, the ability to reflectively consider alternative interpretations of the nonreflective beliefs that seem to support theism is a frontline defense for the atheist. Consequently, formal education may be a critical factor in dissuading someone from theism. Note that this connection between education or reflective contemplation and atheism does not mean that atheists are smarter than theists. Similarly, having the time to contemplatively consider various ideas does not *necessarily* lead to atheism. Plenty of atheist scholars have actually reflectively found their way to theism. My point is that the naturalness of religion may be discouraged by the artificial (meaning human-made) pursuit of knowledge.

Finally, industrialization, urbanization, and the development of educational systems have encouraged advances in sciences and technologies. Science is a double-edged sword for religious thought. On one side, science has documented the wonderful complexity of our universe, our world, and ourselves, enhancing the powerful urge to see it all as designed by an intelligent being. On the other side, phenomena previously understood only in terms of the activity of gods now can be understood either in completely naturalistic terms or in some complex combination of natural and divine causes. Technology has provided humans with more and more power to impact natural forces. Humans can create marvelous things and inflict horrible destruction. At one point in history, a shiny silver object flying through the sky was a dead-ringer for the work of a god. Now it is the commonplace activity of humans. The obliteration of Sodom and Gomorrah by fire from heaven could only have been an act of God. The similar annihilation of Hiroshima and Nagasaki could only have been the act of humans.

But perhaps sciences greatest assault on theism has not come from the truths people have gained through it or the technologies produced by it. Rather, our faith in the sciences has spawned *scientism*, a worldview dedicated to the notion that science ultimately can answer all questions and solve all problems. Though science cannot really explain why the universe is fine-tuned to support intelligent life or why we *should* behave morally, perhaps some day it will. This unbridled optimism in the power of science finds faithful followers among many educated citizens of urban Australia, Canada, Europe, and the United States, though professional scientists and philosophers of science tend to be less sanguine than intellectuals a step or two removed from the art. Scientism serves as a reflective safety net for atheists. As I have argued, theists do not believe in God because of apparent design in the universe, but belief in design finds a mutually supportive match with the idea of God. However, issues such as apparent design may be problematic for atheists unless they have a device such as scientism to assure them that even if they do not personally have a satisfactory explanation for apparent design, surely science either has one or will come up with one.

To summarize, atheism has a chance to emerge and spread only among the more privileged members of the developed nations of the world—in Europe and North America particularly. As a testament to its naturalness, even in places where oppressive, totalitarian regimes have tried to crush theism, such as in China or the former Soviet Union, theism remains strong, though hidden, among common folk. Only privileged minorities enjoy atheism. If religion is the opiate of the masses, atheism is a luxury of the elite. This may be especially true of academics not because we are so much smarter (though we like to think so) or so scientifically minded (a higher proportion of physicists than sociologists are theists) but because we enjoy an environment especially designed to short-circuit intuitive judgments tied to natural day-to-day demands and experiences. This is why atheism may seem so natural to those in the academy when evidence suggests otherwise. To adapt a simile from anthropologist and developmental psychologist Larry Hirschfeld, atheist academics marveling about how strange it is for people to be religious is a bit like two-headed people discovering one-headed people and thinking how odd *they* are. Religious belief is the natural backdrop to the oddity that is atheism.

Notes

1. For a fairly contemporary version of such an argument that avoids many traditional pitfalls, see Swinburne (1992).

2. Much of the cosmological work that details the fine-tuned nature of the universe has been captured under the "anthropic principle" (Leslie, 1982, 1983; see also Carter, 2002).

3. International Social Survey Program (1991).

In Conclusion

A T THE CONCLUSION of the conference that inspired this book's writing, the organizer hosted the presenters and a small number of others at a nice dinner. Slow service left plenty of time for conversation. At one point, someone asked another of the presenters and I whether it wasn't the case that the reason people grew up believing in God was fear. Couldn't you get kids to believe almost any idea that couldn't be disproven if the consequence for disbelieving was eternal damnation and perhaps a thorough beating in the meantime? I found this question noteworthy for at least two reasons. First, it showed that I had not been clear enough in my presentation. This very intelligent professor had missed a crucial point of the argument and was left believing that all that is required for a religious belief is for the belief to be nonprovable or disprovable by scientific means. Second, the question betrayed a bias that belief in God is so peculiar, so hard to believe, that surely it must take coercion or other drastic measures for anyone to believe. I hope that in writing this book I have righted both of these misconceptions.

What Makes a God?

Religious concepts—specifically god concepts—cannot be just any old strange ideas, and being nonfalsifiable is *not* their distinguishing feature. Many nonreligious beliefs we hold near and dear cannot be proven or disproven. Rather, god concepts tend to be distinguished by a number of ways in which they capitalize on ordinary mental structures to gain their strong ability to spread from person to person and generation to generation and to be believed. First, god concepts meet the vast majority of the assumptions of mental tools, making them easy to remember and understand, but they violate a small number—maybe just one or two—of these intuitive assumptions in any given day-to-day context. As described in chapter 2, these small tweaks may make these minimally counterintuitive concepts attention demanding and possessing great ability to generate explanations, predictions, and inferences.

Second, the central religious ideas revolve around intentional agents—beings that can initiate action and not merely respond to environmental contingencies. Gods, then, are minimally counterintuitive agents. By virtue of being agents, gods enjoy tremendous inferential potential but also play into the hyperactivity of a particular mental tool, the hypersensitive agency detection device (HADD). In chapter 3, I offered that this mental tool finds agents and agency in the environment given scant information, and sometimes these agent detections match god concepts that have been floated in a population. When this sort of match occurs, people gain more reasons for belief. And under very special conditions, HADD may even lead to the postulation of a god to account for an experience. So, then, religious beliefs that amount to minimally counterintuitive agent concepts stand a greater likelihood of being spread and believed.

In chapter 4, I suggested that by being agents with one or two counterintuitive properties (such as reading minds or being invisible), gods may be easily invoked in matters of social concern. As beings that may know strategic information about others or oneself, gods demand our attention as potential enemies or allies. Likewise, possessing a god's-eye view enables gods to know the truth about moral disputes—who has been truly wronged and who has been behaving treacherously. Thus, gods may be invoked in matters of moral dispute or be claimed as the causes of unusual fortune or misfortune that may be payment for moral triumph or failure.

These biases concerning how mental tools operate in the ordinary world encourage the spread of belief in gods and thus characterize, at least in part, what we call "gods." If someone advanced religious beliefs without these features, they would not compete as well for space in human minds, all else being equal. A god cannot be any strange idea that cannot be proven wrong. Rather, gods fall into a very narrow range of concepts with peculiar features making them highly transmitted and likely to be believed. An even narrower range of god concepts enjoy enhanced credibility and transmission because of their fit with developing mental tools in children. As discussed in chapter 6, gods that happen to be superpowerful, superknowing, superperceiving, and immortal may find fertile soil in the minds of children particularly, encouraging their vertical transmission. Hence, God of the Abrahamic traditions may be one of the more well-suited god concepts for cultural survival.

Could Coercion Be the Driving Force?

By now it should be clear that I see no need for threats of hell or punitive measures for convincing people to believe in God as my colleague at the conference dinner suggested. The threat of eternal damnation or other punishment for disbelief is not a common thread in broadly theistic belief systems and does not even occur consistently in Christianity. Further, we have no evidence that abusive action could actually teach someone to believe "any old" counterintuitive, nonprovable concept.

Take an example. Suppose that the adults in a small town claimed that one of the schoolteachers stopped existing every Wednesday unless someone was looking at her. Certainly this concept is a counterintuitive agent concept. Such a claim cannot be disproved (any attempt to do so would lead the teacher to *not* stop existing and behave normally). And suppose that adults told the children that if they did not believe, they would be beaten and then turn into worms when they died. Would we expect the children to come to believe this claim? Not hardly. Such a concept has poor inferential potential and does not hold the promise of working its way into the natural thinking of day-to-day life. As such, it has a poor nonreflective foundation. What we might expect is that children of this town will *claim* to believe in their peculiar teacher out of fear but hold no true belief.

The idea that religious belief is spread by aggressive or violent threats isn't wholly the result of antitheistic bias, but it has some root in Western history. After all, didn't Spanish, Portuguese, French, Dutch, and English Christians brutally force indigenous peoples in Asia, Africa, and the Americas to become Christians? The history of Christian expansion contains numerous shameful episodes that would have undoubtedly disgusted the faith's founder. However, the forced spread of both Islam and Christianity represent cases of one theism replacing or being added to others and not the wholesale imposition of theism on atheists. Thus, appeal to these historical dynamics may help explain only the distribution of particular religious beliefs but not religious beliefs themselves.

What about Mystical Experiences?

Sometimes when colleagues or I finish speaking about the cognitive science of religion, we also get questions concerning the role of mystical religious experiences. Such questions generally arise because of scholarly and not personal concerns. Since William James, the study of special, mystical religious experience has been a staple of the psychological study of religion.[1] In contrast, very few people—believers or not—report having "peak" experiences, and such experiences have not been convincingly linked to the prevalence of religious belief in a community. That is, people do not typically believe in God because of a personal encounter with the Divine. If these special religious experiences do figure into belief in God, it is through the means I described in chapter 3. Because of their character or because of externally offered interpretations, these experiences excite HADD and the Theory of Mind (ToM) tool, thereby enhancing existing belief or priming for future belief. "Experiencing God" does not happen in a conceptual vacuum.[2]

Putting Things in Perspective

Throughout my career in American academic circles I repeatedly discovered that scientistic devotion and living in just the sort of elitist, artificial environment described in chapter 8 rendered many of my colleagues unable to see the naturalness of religious belief. My point in this book is fairly simple: widespread belief in God arises from the operation of natural processes of the human mind in ordinary human environments. Belief in God does not amount to anything strange or peculiar; on the contrary, such belief is nearly inevitable. I have simply tried to put belief in God in perspective.

At points in my argument, especially in chapters 7 and 8, atheist readers might have felt uncomfortable: Does he really mean that atheism is unnatural? Abnormal? Yes. Counting noses, especially from a historical perspective, shows that atheism constitutes a small minority position. I maintain that atheism requires a narrow band of environmental conditions in order to thrive, and these environmental conditions must be deliberately produced by human activity. In contrast, theism finds almost all human environments fertile. The idea of a supreme God, as in that of the Abrahamic traditions, may be particularly prodigious, as the rapid spread of these faiths over the last two millennia demonstrates.

On the other hand, heroic or horrific efforts have been required to strip people of their religious beliefs. Communist and socialist totalitarian regimes around the world have struggled in vain to eradicate religious belief but have succeeded mostly in driving religious commitments "underground." Where atheism has relished its greatest triumphs has been among the privileged nations of the world with their higher-education institutions that systematically starve and sometimes directly attack religious belief through ridicule and even censorship. On numerous occasions, I have heard professors at state-funded universities in the United States exclaim in front of students, "How could anyone believe in these absurd religious ideas?" Of course, students do not line up to be counted as absurd by their professors.

I hope this book has offered an answer to these colleagues' exasperation. I also hope I have shown that religious belief may be comparable to other beliefs that many of these befuddled professors hold near and dear, such as belief in other people's minds, belief in the permanence of physical principles governing our world, and belief in moral certitudes. Grounds for dismissing the existence of God (or gods) must be stronger than observing that God's existence cannot be scientifically proven or disproven or that many of the phenomena explained by appealing to God in the past now may be "explained" scientifically. Such criteria for dismissing belief would destroy many core beliefs along with belief in God.

Though I may have placed atheism in a more defensive stance (in terms of naturalness), to many the argument I have presented here (and in other works on the naturalness of religion) may seem like a brutal and effective attack on theism. After my presentations, some antitheists have walked away with broad smiles and feelings of self-satisfaction: "See. Religion really is all in believers' heads! They only believe because of the peculiarities of the human mind. But with enough effort, education, and resources, this ignorance may be overcome." Likewise, theists sometimes find the suggestion that belief in God may be traced to *evolved* functions of the mind–brain offensive and completely off base.

Other implications, however, may be drawn. The account I have given for why people believe in God is entirely consistent with some theologies. I was once riding on a train in India, chatting with a fellow in my car. At one point, I shared with him my then-new experimental results that showed that kids may be able to effectively reason about God's properties (chapter 6) but that sometimes adults seem to have great difficulty keeping God's superproperties straight (as in the narrative comprehension task described in chapter 1). To my surprise, the man immediately replied, "Do you want to know why?" He proceeded to explain that children have recently been with the Divine, and so their belief and understanding is pure. But through living in this world, adult belief becomes corrupted. In other words, belief in God comes naturally. Disbelief requires human intervention.

Some Christians, myself included, offer a similar account. God created people with the capability to know and love him but with the free will to reject him. Consequently, our God-endowed nature leads us to believe, but human endeavors apart from God's design may result in disbelief. Even if this natural tendency toward belief in God can be conclusively demonstrated to be the work of evolved capacities, Christians need not be deterred. God may have fine-tuned the cosmos to allow for life and for evolution and then orchestrated mutations and selection to produce the sort of organisms we are—evolution through "supernatural selection."

These observations should reveal that I find the cognitive science of religion independent of whether someone *should* or *should not* believe in God. Whether God (or most other gods) exists cannot be proven or disproven by science.[3] Metaphysical concerns such as this remain in the domain of philosophy. Nevertheless, as with all fields able to uncover facts of the material world, certain religious positions may be more or less consistent with the findings of the cognitive science of religion and thus more or less rationally justifiable. A faith, for instance, that teaches that religious belief arises only through mystical experience or can be attained only by adults or through special training or skills would be a faith incommensurate with the facts.

On the other hand, those who attack any and all religious beliefs would be advised to be sure that their attacks square with the facts. Belief in God or gods does not arise because of peculiar brain states or psychological abnormalities. A god cannot be any grab bag of concepts a charismatic leader wishes it to be. Belief in God or gods is not some artificial intrusion into the natural state of human affairs. Rather, belief in gods generally and God particularly arises through the natural, ordinary operation of human minds in natural ordinary environments.

Why would anyone believe in God? The design of our minds leads us to believe.

Notes

1. James 1972 (1902).

2. An unusual experience that leads some people to claim they have been touched by God might just as well lead others to believe they need a little less stress in their lives and a little more sleep. Investigations of the neurological substrate supporting religious experiences have begun receiving a fair amount of attention (Newberg and D'Aquilli, 1998; Persinger, 1995; Persinger, 1999). Most of this work attempts to isolate religious experiences in particular neurological structures and processes. But insofar as experiences require conceptual processing for the experiences to become relevant to religious belief or action, it is the conceptual processing I am interested in. I see the most exciting prospects for the neuroscience of religion as identifying the parts of the brain that house this processing.

3. Theological formulations of God's properties render God's existence outside of scientific inquiry because science is concerned with the measurable material world. Nevertheless, formulating a god concept that would fall under scientific scrutiny is possible. Suppose someone said that a god lived at the top of Mount Olympus sitting in a chair, never left Mount Olympus, and was visible to the unaided human eye, so that if you climbed Mount Olympus, you would see the god. Under this theological description, one could certainly investigate whether the theological claim was true. Few lasting theologies are built on these sorts of falsifiable empirical claims.

Glossary

Agency Detection Device (ADD) (Categorizer)—A mental tool that determines whether an object is an agent or whether some event or trace is the result of agency. In many contexts, ADD may detect agency given only scant information; hence, it may also be termed the hypersensitive agency detection device.

Agent—A being that does not merely respond mechanistically to environmental contingencies but initiates action on the basis of internal, mental states.

Animal Identifier (Categorizer)—A mental tool responsible for determining whether an object is an animal and communicating this nonreflective belief to the living-thing describer.

Artifact Describer (Describer)—A mental tool that registers nonreflective beliefs concerning the properties of an artifact, as determined by the artifact identifier.

Artifact Identifier (Categorizer)—A mental tool responsible for determining whether an object is human-made.

Categorizers—A class of largely nonconscious mental tools that identify an object or substance on the basis of its perceived properties. Categorizers form nonreflective beliefs about the identities of things and sort them into groups. Categorizers include the agency detection device, the animal identifier, the artifact identifier, the face detector, and the object detection device. Categorizers communicate primarily with each other and with describers.

Describers—A class of largely nonconscious mental tools generating nonreflective beliefs concerning the properties of various sorts of things. Describers include the artifact describer, the living-thing describer, the object describer, and the Theory of Mind tool.

Face Detector (Categorizer)—A mental tool that determines whether a pattern in the environment is a human face.

Facilitators—A class of mental tools that help people negotiate social interactions. Operating primarily on detected agents and often their presumed mental states in particular contexts, facilitators rely heavily on the operation of the agency detection device and the Theory of Mind tool. Facilitators include intuitive morality, the social exchange regulator, and the social status monitor.

Gods—Any minimally counterintuitive agents believed in by a community of people for which there are observable behavioral consequences of the belief.

Hypersensitive Agency Detection Device (HADD)—*See* Agency Detection Device.

Intuitive Morality (Facilitator)—A mental tool that generates thoughts and feelings concerning how people *should* behave, giving rise to moral codes.

Living-Thing Describer (Describer)—A mental tool that forms nonreflective beliefs concerning the properties of a living thing detected by other mental tools.

Mental Tools—Functional systems of the mind–brain that handle specific processing problems. The adult mind is not a general processing device but (either through development and/or biological biases) consists of specialized subsystems. Many mental tools operate without conscious awareness.

Minimally Counterintuitive (MCI)—Concepts that match up with the intuitive properties of a sort of thing but include a small number of violations of expectations. Though the number of violations is not precisely known, it seems that one or two in any one context serve as a limit. Being minimally counterintuitive endows a concept with greater likelihood of being remembered and faithfully transmitted.

Nonreflective Belief—A belief that is not consciously held and that is generated by the functioning of mental tools. Nonreflective beliefs guide many day-to-day activities without our awareness and free our conscious minds to perform other tasks. Much of what may be considered intuitive knowledge consists of nonreflective beliefs.

Object Describer (Describer)—A mental tool that generates assumptions concerning the properties of physical objects once the object is identified by the object detection device.

Object Detection Device (ODD) (Categorizer)—A mental tool that uses sensory-perceptual information to determine the presence of a bounded, physical object.

Reflective Belief—A belief that is consciously held and accessible to conscious reflection. Many reflective beliefs arise through the nonconscious tabulation of nonreflective beliefs.

Rituals—Following Lawson and McCauley (1990) and McCauley and Lawson (2002), an event during which an agent acts on someone or something to bring about a state of affairs that would not naturally follow from the action. A religious ritual further requires the presence of a superhuman agent being included somewhere in the ritual or previous prerequisite rituals.

Theory of Mind (ToM)—A mental tool that generates descriptions and makes predictions about the mental activities, including beliefs, desires, emotions, perceptions, opinions, and attitudes, of others and self. ToM is a describer that operates on agents detected by the agency detection device.

Transmission—The spread of an idea or concept from one mind to another. For a concept to be "cultural" or "religious," it must be relatively faithfully transmitted to the minds of numerous people in a group.

Sensory Pageantry—A term coined by McCauley and Lawson (2002) referring to the amount of sensory excitement and emotionality generated by a religious ritual observance.

Social Exchange Regulator (Facilitator)—A mental tool concerned with tracking social exchanges, including who owes what to whom and what social obligations must be met before something else may take place.

Social Status Monitor (Facilitator)—A mental tool that attends to the relative status of people in a group in order to determine the attractiveness of others for association and to serve as models from which to learn.

References

Aronson, E. (Ed.). 1999. *The social animal* (8th ed.). New York: Worth.

Atran, S. (2002). *In gods we trust: The evolutionary landscape of religion.* Oxford: Oxford University Press.

Banaji, M. R., & Bhaskar, R. (2000). Implicit stereotypes and memory: The bounded rationality of social beliefs. In D. L. Schacter & E. Scarry (Eds.), *Memory, brain, and belief* (pp. 139–175). Cambridge, MA: Harvard University Press.

Banaji, M. R., & Greenwald, A. G. (1994). Implicit stereotyping and prejudice. In M. P. Zanna & J. M. Olson (Eds.), *The psychology of prejudice: The Ontario Symposium* (Vol. 7, pp. 55–76). Hillsdale, NJ: Erlbaum.

Baron-Cohen, S. (1995). *Mindblindness: An essay on autism and theory of mind.* Cambridge, MA: MIT Bradford.

Baron-Cohen, S. (2002). The extreme male brain theory of autism. *Trends in Cognitive Sciences, 6,* 248–254.

Barrett, J. L. (1998). Cognitive constraints on Hindu concepts of the divine. *Journal for the Scientific Study of Religion, 37,* 608–619.

Barrett, J. L. (1999). Theological correctness: Cognitive constraint and the study of religion. *Method and Theory in the Study of Religion, 11,* 325–339.

Barrett, J. L. (2000). Exploring the natural foundations of religion. *Trends in Cognitive Sciences, 4,* 29–34.

Barrett, J. L. (2001). How ordinary cognition informs petitionary prayer. *Journal of Cognition and Culture, 1,* 259–269.

Barrett, J. L. (2003). Bringing data to mind: Empirical claims of Lawson and McCauley's theory of religious ritual. In B. C. Wilson & T. Light (Eds.), *Religion as a human sacrifice: A Festschrift in honor of E. Thomas Lawson* (pp. 265–288). Leiden: Brill.

Barrett, J. L., & Johnson, A. H. (2003). Research note: The role of control in attributing intentional agency to inanimate objects. *Journal of Cognition and Culture, 3,* 208–217.

Barrett, J. L., & Keil, F. C. (1996). Anthropomorphism and god concepts: Conceptualizing a non-natural entity. *Cognitive Psychology, 31,* 219–247.

Barrett, J. L., Newman, R., & Richert, R. A. (2003). When seeing does not lead to believing: Children's understanding of the importance of background knowledge for interpreting visual displays. *Journal of Cognition and Culture, 3,* 91–108.

Barrett, J. L., & Nyhof, M. A. (2001). Spreading non-natural concepts: The role of intuitive conceptual structures in memory and transmission of cultural materials. *Journal of Cognition and Culture, 1,* 69–100.

Barrett, J. L., & Richert, R. A. (2003). Anthropomorphism or preparedness? Exploring children's concept of God. *Review of Religious Research, 44,* 300–312.

Barrett, J. L., Richert, R. A., & Driesenga, A. (2001). God's beliefs versus mother's: The development of non-human agent concepts. *Child Development, 71,* 50–65.

Barrett, J. L., & Van Orman, B. (1996). The effects of image use in worship on God concepts. *Journal of Psychology and Christianity, 15,* 38–45.

Barth, F. (1975). *Ritual and knowledge among the Baktaman of New Guinea.* New Haven, CT: Yale University Press.

Bassili, J. (1976). Temporal and spatial contingencies in the perception of social events. *Journal of Personality and Social Psychology, 33,* 680–685.

Bateson, C. D. (1975). Rational processing or rationalization? The effect of disconfirming information on a stated religious belief. *Journal of Personality and Social Psychology, 32,* 176–184.

Bering, J. (2002). Intuitive conceptions of dead agents' minds: The natural foundations of afterlife beliefs as phenomenological boundary. *Journal of Cognition and Culture, 2,* 263–308.

Berry, D., Misovich, P., Keen, R., & Baron, S. (1992). Effects of disruption of structure and motion on perceptions of social causality. *Personality and Social Psychology Bulletin, 18,* 237–244.

Bloom, P. (1998). Theories of artifact categorization. *Cognition, 66,* 87–93.

Boyer, P. (1993). Cognitive aspects of religious symbolism. In P. Boyer (Ed.), *Cognitive aspects of religious symbolism* (pp. 4–47). Cambridge: Cambridge University Press.

Boyer, P. (1994). *The naturalness of religious ideas: A cognitive theory of religion.* Berkeley: University of California Press.

Boyer, P. (1995). Causal understandings in cultural representations: Cognitive constraints on inferences from cultural input. In D. Sperber, D. Premack, & A. J. Premack (Eds.), *Causal cognition: A multidisciplinary debate.* Oxford: Clarendon Press.

Boyer, P. (1996). What makes anthropomorphism natural: Intuitive ontology and cultural representations. *Journal of the Royal Anthropological Institute (N.S.), 2,* 83–97.

Boyer, P. (1998). Cognitive tracks of cultural inheritance: How evolved intuitive ontology governs cultural transmission. *American Anthropologist, 100,* 876–889.

Boyer, P. (2000). Evolution of a modern mind and the origins of culture: Religious concepts as a limiting case. In P. Carruthers & A. Chamberlain (Eds.), *Evolution and the human mind: Modularity, language and meta-cognition* (pp. 93–112). Cambridge: Cambridge University Press.

Boyer, P. (2001). *Religion explained: The evolutionary origins of religious development.* New York: Basic Books.

Boyer, P., & Ramble, C. (2001). Cognitive templates for religious concepts: Cross-cultural evidence for recall of counter-intuitive representations. *Cognitive Science*, 25, 535–564.

Boyer, P., & Walker, S. (2000). Intuitive ontology and cultural input in the acquisition of religious concepts. In K. S. Rosengren, C. N. Johnson, & P. L. Harris (Eds.), *Imagining the impossible: Magical, scientific, and religious thinking in children* (pp. 130–156). Cambridge: Cambridge University Press.

Brown, R., & Kulik, J. (1982). Flashbulb memory. In U. Neisser (Ed.), *Memory observed: Remembering in natural contexts.* San Francisco: W. H. Freeman.

Carruthers, P., & Smith, P. K. (Eds.). (1996). *Theories of theories of mind.* Cambridge: Cambridge University Press.

Carter, B. (2002). Large number of coincidences and the anthropic principle in cosmology. In M. S. Longair (Ed.), *Confrontation of cosmological theories with observational data* (pp. 291–298). Dordrecht: Kluwer Academic Publishers.

Clifford, M. M., & Walster, E. H. (1973). The effect of physical attractiveness on teacher expectation. *Sociology of Education*, 46, 248–258.

Cosmides, L. (1989). The logic of social exchange: Has natural selection shaped how humans reason? Studies with the Wason selection task. *Cognition*, 31, 187–276.

Cosmides, L., & Tooby, J. (1989). Evolutionary psychology and the generation of culture: II. Case study: A computational theory of social exchange. *Ethology and Sociobiology*, 10, 51–97.

Cosmides, L., Tooby, J., & Barkow, J. (1992). Evolutionary psychology and conceptual integration. In J. Barkow, L. Cosmides, & J. Tooby (Eds.), *The adapted mind: Evolutionary psychology and the generation of culture.* New York: Oxford University Press.

Dion, K. K. (1972). Physical attractiveness and evaluations of children's transgressions. *Journal of Personality and Social Psychology*, 24, 207–213.

Evans, E. M. (2001). Cognitive and contextual factors in the emergence of diverse belief systems: Creation versus evolution. *Cognitive Psychology*, 42, 217–266.

Festinger, L. (1957). *A theory of cognitive dissonance.* Stanford, CA: Stanford University Press.

Festinger, L., & Carlsmith, J. M. (1959). Cognitive consequences of forced compliance. *Journal of Abnormal and Social Psychology*, 58, 203–210.

Gelman, R., Durgin, F., & Kaufman, L. (1995). Distinguishing between animates and inanimates: Not by motion alone. In D. Sperber, D. Premack, & A. J. Premack (Eds.), *Causal cognition: A multidisciplinary debate* (pp. 150–184). Oxford: Clarendon Press.

Gergely, G., & Csibra, G. (2003). Teleological reasoning in infancy: The naïve theory of rational action. *Trends in Cognitive Sciences*, 7, 287–292.

Gergely, G., Nadasdy, Z., Csibra, G., & Biro, S. (1995). Taking the intentional stance at 12 months of age. *Cognition*, 56, 165–193.

Gilovich, T. (1991). *How we know what isn't so: The fallibility of human reason in everyday life.* New York: Free Press.

Gimenez, M., Guerrero, S., & Harris, P. L. (in press). *Understanding the impossible: Intimations of immortality and omniscience in early childhood.*

Goldman, A. (1992). In defense of the simulation theory. *Mind and Language*, 7, 104–119.

Gordon, R. M. (1986). Folk psychology as simulation. *Mind and Language*, 1, 158–171.

Gordon, R. M. (1992). The simulation theory: Objections and misconceptions. *Mind and Language*, 7, 11–34.

Guthrie, S. E. (1993). *Faces in the clouds: A new theory of religion.* New York: Oxford University Press.

Hacking, I. (1987). The inverse gambler's fallacy: The argument from design. The anthropic principle applied to wheeler universes. *Mind, 96,* 331–340.

Happe, F. G. E. (1995). The role of age and verbal ability in the theory of mind task performance of subjects with autism. *Child Development, 66,* 843–855.

Happe, F. G. E., Winner, E., & Brownell, H. (1998). The getting of wisdom: Theory of mind in old age. *Developmental Psychology, 34,* 358–362.

Harris, P. L. (1992). From simulation to folk psychology: The case for development. *Mind and Language,* 7, 120–144.

Heider, F., & Simmel, M. (1944). An experimental study of apparent behavior. *American Journal of Psychology, 57,* 243–249.

Henrich, J., and Gil-White, F. (2001). The evolutions of prestige: Freely conferred deference as a mechanism for enhancing the benefits of cultural transmission. *Evolution and Human Behavior, 22,* 165–196.

Hirschfeld, L. A. (1994a). The child's representation of human groups. In D. Medin (Ed.), *The psychology of learning and motivation: Advances in research and theory* (Vol. 31, pp. 133–185). San Diego: Academic Press.

Hirschfeld, L. A. (1994b). Is the acquisition of social categories based on domain-specific competence or knowledge transfer? In L. Hirschfeld & S. Gelman (Eds.), *Mapping the mind: Domain specificity in cognition* (pp. 201–233). New York: Cambridge University Press.

Hirschfeld, L. A. (1995). Anthropology, psychology, and the meanings of social causality. In D. Sperber, D. Premack, & A. J. Premack (Eds.), *Causal cognition: A multidisciplinary debate* (pp. 313–350). New York: Oxford University Press.

Hirschfeld, L. A., & Gelman, S. A. (Eds.). (1994). *Mapping the mind: Domain specificity in cognition and culture.* Cambridge: Cambridge University Press.

International Social Survey Program (1991). International Social Survey Program: Religion [Computer file]. Cologne Germany: Zentralarchiv für empirische Sozialforschung [producer], 1993. Cologne Germany: Zentralarchiv für empirische Sozialforschung; Ann Arbor, MI: Interuniversity Consortium for Political and Social Research [distributors], 1994.

James, W. (1972 [1902]). *Varieties of religious experience.* London: Fontana Press.

Katz, L. D. (Ed.). (2000). *Evolutionary origins of morality: Cross-disciplinary perspectives.* Thoverton, UK: Imprint Academic.

Keil, F. C. (1989). *Concepts, kinds and conceptual development.* Cambridge, MA: MIT Press.

Keil, F. C. (1992). The origins of an autonomous biology. In M. K. Gunnar & M. Maratsos (Eds.), *Modularity and constraints in language and cognition: Minnesota symposia on child psychology* (Vol. 25, pp. 103–137). Hillsdale, NJ: Erlbaum.

Keil, F. C. (1994). The birth and nurturance of concepts by domains: The origins of concepts of living things. In L. Hirschfeld & S. Gelman (Eds.), *Mapping the mind: Domain specificity in cognition* (pp. 234–254). New York: Cambridge University Press.

Keil, F. C. (1995). The growth of causal understandings of natural kinds. In D. Sperber, D. Premack, & A. J. Premack (Eds.), *Causal cognition: A multidisciplinary debate* (pp. 234–267). New York: Oxford University Press.

Kelemen, D. (1999a). Beliefs about purpose: On the origins of teleological thought. In M. Corballis & S. Lea (Eds.), *The descent of mind: Psychological perspectives on hominid evolution* (pp. 278–294). Oxford: Oxford University Press.

Kelemen, D. (1999b). Functions, goals, and intentions: Children's teleological reasoning about objects. *Trends in Cognitive Sciences, 12,* 461–468.

Kelemen, D. (1999c). The scope of teleological thinking in preschool children. *Cognition, 70,* 241–272.

Kelemen, D. (1999d). Why are rocks pointy? Children's preference for teleological explanations of the natural world. *Developmental Psychology, 35,* 1440–1453.

Kelemen, D. (in press). Are children "intuitive theists"? Reasoning about purpose and design in nature. *Psychological Science.*

Knight, N., Sousa, P., Barrett, J. L., & Atran, S. (in press). Children's attributions of beliefs to humans and God: Cross-cultural evidence. *Cognitive Science.*

Lawson, E. T. (1985). *Religions of Africa: Traditions in transformation.* San Francisco: Harper-Collins.

Lawson, E. T., & McCauley, R. N. (1990). *Rethinking religion: Connection, cognition, and Culture.* Cambridge: Cambridge University Press.

Leslie, A. (1995). A theory of agency. In D. Sperber, D. Premack, & A. J. Premack (Eds.), *Causal cognition: A multidisciplinary debate* (pp. 121–149). Oxford: Clarendon Press.

Leslie, J. (1982). Anthropic principle, world ensemble and design. *American Philosophical Quarterly, 20,* 141–151.

Leslie, J. (1983). Observership in cosmology: The anthropic principle. *Mind, 92,* 573–579.

Lewis, C. S. (1944). *The abolition of man.* New York: Macmillan.

Lewis, C. S. (1952). *Mere Christianity.* New York: Macmillan.

McCauley, R. N., & Lawson, E. T. (2002). *Bringing ritual to mind: Psychological foundations of cultural forms.* Cambridge: Cambridge University Press.

McGuire, W. J. (1964). Inducing resistance to persuasion: Some contemporary approaches. In E. F. Borgatta & W. W. Lambert (Eds.), *Advances in experimental social psychology* (Vol. 1). New York: Academic Press.

Meltzoff, A. N., & Moore, M. K. (1983). Newborn infants imitate adult facial gestures. *Child Development, 54,* 702–709.

Meltzoff, A. N., & Moore, M. K. (1989). Imitation in new-born infants: Exploring the range of gestures imitated and the underlying mechanisms. *Developmental Psychology, 25,* 954–962.

Meltzoff, A. N., & Moore, M. K. (1992). Early imitation within a functional framework: The importance of person identity, movement, and development. *Infant Behavior and Development, 15,* 479–505.

Meltzoff, A. N., & Moore, M. K. (1994). Imitation, memory, and the representation of persons. *Infant Behavior and Development, 17,* 83–99.

Michotte, A. (1963). *The perception of causality*. London: Methuen.

Myers, D. (1990). *Social psychology* (3rd ed.). New York: McGraw-Hill.

Neisser, U., & Harsch, N. (1992). Phantom flashbulbs: False recollections of hearing the news about *Challenger*. In E. Winograd & U. Neisser (Eds.), *Affect and accuracy in recall: Studies of "flashbulb" memories* (pp. 9–31). Cambridge: Cambridge University Press.

Neisser, U., Winograd, E., Bergman, E., Schreiber, C., Palmer, S., & Weldon, M. S. (1996). Remembering the earthquake: Direct experience versus hearing the news. *Memory, 4,* 337–357.

Newberg, A. B., & D'Aquili, E. G. (1998). The neuropsychology of spiritual experience. In H. G. Koenig (Ed.), *Handbook of religion and mental health* (pp. 75–94). San Francisco: Academic Press.

Paloutzian, R. F. (1996). *Invitation to the psychology of religion* (2nd ed.). Boston: Allyn & Bacon.

Persinger, M. A. (1995). Out-of-body-like experiences are more probable in people with elevated complex partial epileptic-like signs during periods of enhanced geomagnetic activity: A nonlinear effect. *Perceptual & Motor Skills, 80,* 563–569.

Persinger, M. A. (1999). Near-death experiences and ecstasy: A product of the organization of the human brain. In S. O. Sala (Ed.), *Mind myths: Exploring popular assumptions about the mind and brain* (pp. 85–99). Chichester, UK: Wiley.

Petrovich, O. (1997). Understanding of non-natural causality in children and adults: A case against artificialism. *Psyche en Geloof, 8,* 151–165.

Petrovich, O. (1999). Preschool children's understanding of the dichotomy between the natural and the artificial. *Psychological Reports, 84,* 3–27.

Piaget, J. (1929). *The child's conception of the world*. New York: Harcourt Brace.

Pinker, S. (1997). *How the mind works*. New York: W. W. Norton.

Plantinga, A. (1990). *God and other minds: A study of the rational justification of belief in God*. Ithaca, NY: Cornell University Press.

Premack, D. (1990). The infant's theory of self-propelled objects. *Cognition, 36,* 1–16.

Premack, D., & Premack, A. J. (1995). Intention as psychological cause. In D. Sperber, D. Premack, & A. J. Premack (Eds.), *Causal cognition: A multidisciplinary debate* (pp. 185–199). Oxford: Clarendon Press.

Richert, R. A., & Barrett, J. L. (in press). Do you see what I see? Young children's assumptions about God's perceptual abilities. *International Journal for the Psychology of Religion*.

Rochat, P., Morgan, R., & Carpenter, M. (1997). Young infants' sensitivity to movement information specifying social causality. *Cognitive Development, 12,* 537–561.

Scholl, B. J., & Tremoulet, P. D. (2000). Perceptual causality and animacy. *Trends in Cognitive Sciences, 4,* 299–308.

Simons, D. J., & Keil, F. C. (1995). As abstract to concrete shift in development of biological thought: The insides story. *Cognition, 56,* 129–163.

Slone, D. J. (in press). *Theological incorrectness: Why religious people believe what they shouldn't*. New York: Oxford University Press.

Spelke, E. S. (1991). Physical knowledge in infancy: Reflections on Piaget's theory. In S. Carey & R. Gelman (Eds.), *The epigenesis of mind: Essays on biology and cognition* (pp. 133–169). Hillsdale, NJ: Erlbaum.

Spelke, E. S., Phillips, A., & Woodward, A. L. (1995). Infants' knowledge of object motion and human action. In D. Sperber, D. Premack, & A. J. Premack (Eds.), *Causal cognition: A multidisciplinary debate* (pp. 44–78). New York: Oxford University Press.

Spelke, E. S., & Van de Walle, G. (1993). Perceiving and reasoning about objects: Insights from infants. In N. Eilan, W. Brewer, & R. McCarthy (Eds.), *Spatial representation* (pp. 132–161). New York: Blackwell.

Sperber, D. (1997). Intuitive and reflective beliefs. *Mind and Language, 12*, 67–83.

Sperber, D., Premack, D., & Premack, A. J. (Eds.). (1995). *Causal cognition: A multidisciplinary debate*. Oxford: Oxford University Press.

Sperber, D., & Wilson, D. (1995). *Relevance: Communication and cognition*. Oxford: Blackwell.

Swinburne, R. G. (1992). The argument from design. In B. A. Brody (Ed.), Readings in the philosophy of Religion: An analytic approach (2nd ed., pp. 189–201). Englewood Cliffs, NJ: Prentice Hall.

Tooby, J., & Cosmides, L. (1992). The psychological foundations of culture. In J. Barkow, L. Cosmides, & J. Tooby (Eds.), *The adapted mind: Evolutionary psychology and the generation of culture* (pp. 163–228). New York: Oxford University Press.

Tremlin, T. (2002). A theory of religious modulation: Reconciling religious modes and ritual arrangements. *Journal of Cognition and Culture, 2*, 309–348.

Turiel, E. (1998). The development of morality. In W. Damon (Ed.), *Handbook of child psychology* (5th ed., Vol. 3, pp. 863–932). New York: Wiley.

Wellman, H., Cross, D., & Watson, J. (2001). Meta-analysis of theory of mind development: The truth about false-belief. *Child Development, 72*, 655–684.

White, P. A. (1995). *The understanding of causation and the production of action*. Hillsdale, NJ: Erlbaum.

White, P. A., & Milne, A. (1999). Impressions of enforced disintegration and bursting in the visual perception of collision events. *Journal of Experimental Psychology: General, 128*, 499–516.

Whitehouse, H. (1995). *Inside the cult: Religious innovation and transmission in Papua New Guinea*. Oxford: Clarendon Press.

Whitehouse, H. (1996a). Apparitions, orations, and rings: Experience of spirits in Dadul. In J. Mageo & A. Howard (Eds.), *Spirits in culture, history, and mind* (pp. 173–193). New York: Routledge.

Whitehouse, H. (1996b). Rites of terror: Emotion, metaphor, and memory in Melanesian initiation cults. *Journal of the Royal Anthropological Institute, 2*, 703–715.

Whitehouse, H. (2000). *Arguments and icons: Divergent modes of religiosity*. Oxford: Oxford University Press.

Whitehouse, H. (2004). *Modes of religiosity: A cognitive theory of religious transmission*. Walnut Creek, CA: AltaMira Press.

Wilson, D. S. (2002). *Darwin's cathedral: Evolution, religion, and the nature of society*. Chicago: University of Chicago Press.

Index

Page numbers in *italics* refer to tables.

About the Author

After completing his Ph.D. in experimental psychology at Cornell University, Justin L. Barrett served on the psychology faculties of Calvin College and the University of Michigan, Ann Arbor, and as a research fellow of the Institute for Social Research. Recently, he was the associate director for the International Culture and Cognition Consortium and an editor of the *Journal of Cognition and Culture*. His cross-cultural, developmental, and experimental research on religious concepts has appeared in numerous books and scholarly journals. Dr. Barrett currently provides consulting on numerous research and evaluation projects for academic and nonprofit groups, especially concerning the interface of science and religion.